*To Priscilla,
thanks for the
and support,*
Jana`Chantel

INTO MY MIND

Jana`Chantel

Into My Mind © 2011 by My Vision Works Publishing
Farmington Hills, MI 48334

Contributors:
Book Interior and Cover Design-My Vision Works Publishing

Editor-in-Chief-Rhonda Boggess
Senior Editor: Liz Marabeas

All rights reserved. No part of this book may be reproduced or transmitted in any form or by any means, electronic or mechanical, including information storage and retrieval systems, without permission in writing from the publisher.

Printed in the United States of America.

ISBN-13: 978-1456415280
ISBN-10: 145641528X

Library of Congress Cataloging-in-Publication Data

Chantel, Jana`

Into My Mind by Jana` Chantel

1. Non-fiction
2. African-American
3. Women

For marketing and publicity, please send email to:
janachatel@yahoo.com

www.myvsionsworkspublishing.com

Special thanks to my soul-friend and writing partner Teresa, who provided critiques, took late night e-mails and phone calls just to help me get this book together. A special thanks to my family and friends who never for a second doubted me or my talent and told me that there were no limits to where I can go. A special thanks to my writing professors at Grand Valley State University who took my e-mails and phone calls to provide me feedback, even after I graduated. And, most importantly, I thank God. Without him I wouldn't be where I am today. Lord I thank you.

*I dedicate this book to my parents,
I'm just trying to the things you never got the
chance to do.*

*R.I.P.
Gwen Felicia
And
James Cardell White*

*"It is the mind that maketh good or ill,
That maketh wretch or happy, rich or poor."*

EDMUND SPENSER, The Faerie Queene

CONTENTS

Paranoia _____ 1

A Part of Me I Left Behind _____ 16

The Great Adventure of Jana` Chantel's Death _____ 22

Because They Said That Good Things Will Come To Those Who Wait _____ 36

Still Waiting For Good Things To Come _____ 52

Death, Death and More Death _____ 67

Things My Father Taught Me _____ 76

Like Mother, Like Daughter: A Case Study of Love ___ 89

Things Left Unsaid _____ 104

This Scar of Mine _____ 113

Paranoia

I stood there helplessly as I watched the young girl kicking, screaming, and rolling around on her living room floor. She was in pain—that was certain. The burning, tingling feeling overwhelmed her. It felt like a fire entered her body; a strong vibration ripped through her. She kept grabbing her right leg as if she couldn't feel it anymore. I desperately wanted to console her. I wanted to kneel down by her side and gently rub her head, while telling her that everything was going to be ok. But everything was not ok. It was far from it...

I open my eyes. Back to reality. I am lying on the living room floor—just like the young girl. I feel that burning, tingling feeling—just like the young girl. And I can't feel my right leg—just like the young girl. Then, I realize that I *am* that young girl. I try to remember what all happened before this event:

1. I was babysitting my little sister Autumn.
2. I was getting Erica, my junior high friend, something to drink.
3. I was talking in the living room with my brother, James, and Erica.
4. James said something funny.
5. There was a loud popping noise.
6. I saw fire.

G

My worst fear is that I will die like my mother. I pray to God that he will let me die peacefully. I don't want to be killed like my mother was. But, the weird thing is my mother died from a gunshot; I almost died from a gunshot—weird, huh?

I feel as if I am haunted by my mother. I constantly have dreams about her death. The pain I experience from watching that night unfold over and over again makes the void inside of me grow bigger and bigger.

**

I stand in the house on St. Mary's—the house where my mother was killed—as my current self. I watch as I, my one-year-old self, sit on the floor. Sometimes I am playing with toys, sometimes I'm just sitting there. My mother walks around the house, attending to things. Washing dishes. Sweeping and moping the floors. Folding clothes. My current self often stands there watching my mother in awe, admiring her beauty. Her light beautiful skin, her long pretty hair, and her beautiful brown eyes. Those eyes, those beautiful brown eyes get me every time.

There's a knock at the front door. Even in my dream, I can feel my asthma acting up. My heart begins to race. I watch as my mother walks to the front door. I follow her frantically.

"No!" I yell to her, "Mama, please don't answer the door."

My one-year-old self continues to sit on the floor, playing with my toys, or just sitting there.

"Who is it?" my mother says.
"Hey, Gwen it's..." I can never catch his name.
"James isn't here," she tells him.
"I know, he told me I could come over here and get something," he lies.
"No Mommy," I say. "He's here to do you harm," but she doesn't hear me. I stand in front of her trying to push her back and block the door. But my attempts are useless; her right hand goes through my stomach, opening the front door.

She opens the door, only to get rushed by three men in baseball caps. They hit on her and tell her to take them to the safe. Tears stream down my face. I watch as the men beat on my mother, demanding the money that is in the safe. Her screams are unbearable. Her screams blend with the screams of my one- year-old self.

Her screams.
    My screams.
        Her screams.
            My screams.
                Her screams.
                    My screams.
                        Hermyscreams.

Screams...I can't take it! My head feels like it's going to explode.

My mother hands them the contents in the safe.
"Please!" I say through tears. "Please just leave her alone. She gave you what you want, please leave her alone." My pleas go unheard.
I watch as the men take my mother to the basement. I keep pleading with them.
"Please leave her alone." They don't hear me.

"Stop! Please, just stop!" They keep beating her.

"Take me instead, PLEASE!!!" I have to save her. I have to do something. I need her. But nothing I do helps. I panic as I watch her walk down the basement stairs.

"NOOO!!!!" I scream out hysterically. I know that she will never walk up those stairs again.

I stand at the top of the stairs, too afraid to go down to watch my mother die. My one-year-old self crawls to the top of the stairs, still crying and screaming. I look down at her. I feel the urge to comfort her. To whisper to her that we will survive this, that this event…this moment will make us stronger in the end. I imagine picking myself up and holding her in my twenty-one-year-old arms.

"Ssshhhh," I would tell her as I rock her in my arms. "It's ok, we'll get through this. We'll survive. Don't cry anymore."

But I do nothing. I just stare blankly down the stairs.

There is a muffled sound.

The men walk back up the stairs. The job is done. My mother is no longer with me. I don't look at them as they pass. I don't want to see their faces. I just continue to stare down the stairs. My one-year-old self tries to crawl down the stairs only to tumble down. She lands in a puddle of my mother's blood. She sits there drenched in my mother's blood, screaming and crying. I just stand at the top of the stairs blankly staring at her.

**

I wake up some nights to see my mother standing over me, watching me sleep. Sometimes she's sitting on the bed; her hand gently lies on my right leg. And sometimes she's lying down right next to me, her arms wrapped around me. Always smiling at me. Always with blood slowly trickling down her head.

I feel like I am going crazy.

I add everything together and the realization of my situation becomes clear. I just got shot. The .25 caliber that my brother had been showing off just went off and shot me. He said something funny. I don't remember exactly what he said, but I knew it was funny because I was laughing before it happened. And then I heard that loud, popping noise. I saw the fire. I felt the vibration rip through my body. All I could hear was my screams.

    My screams.
        My screams.
            My screams.
                Myscreams.
                    Screams.
                        Screams.

At the moment, I don't know where I am shot, but I know that a bullet hit me. I'm thirteen years old and looking at death in the face.

I don't know when they came in, but my older cousins Noland and Javon are running in the house from outside. I begin to calm down.

"Jana`, where did you get shot?" my cousin Javon asked as he kneeled beside me.

I don't know where everyone else is at; all I can focus on is him

"I can't feel my right leg," I tell him.

He looks at my leg. "Jana` I don't see a bullet hole." he says. An eerie feeling comes over me. I sigh and look down at my stomach. There it is. A small bullet hole with a bit of blood coming out of it.

The situation just got worse. I would've felt a little bit of relief if it was my leg, there's a higher percentage of survival, but the stomach holds a lot of important organs and arteries. My chance of survival is slim. I slowly look back up at Javon.

"Javon," I say hesitantly, "I got shot in the stomach."

"Oh, man," he whispers sadly. I can see fear in his eyes. I lay on the living room floor in a daze. I think about death. This is the end. The other noises in the house seem unreal.

"James hurt my Nay-Nay!" my little sister Autumn screams. "James hurt my Nay-Nay!" Tiredness begins to creep up on me. I just want to go to sleep. I don't want to be here. I want to get away. Away from reality.

W

I can never be too trusting of people. My mother's killers were people she trusted, people she knew, people that she grew up with—friends, you can say, and they killed her anyway. So I keep people at a distance, even family members. I only let people in as far as I want them in my life. I am afraid that if I let them get too close then they are able hurt me. I constantly think about different scenarios:

- What if I befriend someone and they end up stabbing me in the back?
- What if they kill me?

- What if I let my guard down and they strike?
- What if they kill me?
- What if I invest so much time into a relationship and they betray me?
- What if they kill me?
- What if they kill me?
- WHAT IF *THEY* KILL *ME*?

I wear a mask every day—a mask that shows no emotion. I can be in so much pain and no one can ever know it by just looking at me. I sit in class at times and I can hear my mother's screams. Then I hear my screams, my thirteen-year-old screams.

Her screams.
    My screams.
        Her screams.
            My screams.
                Her screams.
                    My screams.
                        Hermyscreams.

These are the screams of being shot.

And when I blink I see my mother again being attacked by those men. I see the fire from the gun coming towards me. Anger, pain, and sadness rip through me, but you will never see it.

Most of the time I don't to want admit that I am angry, hurt, or sad. Admitting this makes me feel vulnerable. Showing vulnerability makes me easy prey. I don't want to be easy prey. I keep my guards up, I never let them down.

                This isn't healthy.

**

    I am never too flashy because money is the root of all evil. They killed my mother because of money. Money is what they wanted, money is what they got. So I don't wear expensive designer clothes. No Gucci, Prada, or Loui Vitton. No "iced out" jewelry. And no expensive cars like a Phantom, Jaguar, or Maybach. I feel like, if I possessed these things, I would be a target for robbers. My mother got robbed and that robbery ended her life.

    So when I'm out—or even at home, I always do these things:

- I look over my shoulder. *Checking to see who is behind me and how close or far they are from me.*
- I'm aware of my surroundings. *The street light ahead of me is out. There's a group of guys walking towards me to my left. A girl is a few steps behind me, talking on her cell phone.*
- I pay extra attention to shady looking people. *There's a man in worn-down clothes walking towards me. Pay attention! He's looking at you while going in his pocket.*
- I always have some kind of protection on me. *Mace in my left jacket pocket. Always at the ready.*
- I sleep with a knife under my pillow. *My hand on the handle as I sleep.*

    I *am* paranoid.

The realization of dying overwhelms me. I imagine my family members weeping over my body at my funeral. I see my auntie giving my eulogy, telling everyone how I was a good kid and how I am now in heaven. Heaven.

I begin to pray, "Dear Heavenly Father, please forgive me for all the sins that I may have committed. Please let me enter into your kingdom and allow me to be with my mother and father again. In your name I pray, Amen."

Something in my prayer stands out to me. A light at the end of the tunnel. A silver lining. *Allow me to be with my mother and father again...*

Allow me to be with my mother again.

E

I have a fear of having children. My mother died when I was one. My mother's mother died when she was eleven. Notice a pattern? I am afraid that this is some kind of curse and I too will die when my child is young. I don't want that. I want to be a part of my child's life. There are so many things that I want to experience with my child:

- ❖ First steps:
  We're sitting on the living room floor. My husband holds our child in his hands. Our child smiles at me. I smile back and extend out my arms.

"Come to mommy," I say, "Come to mommy." Our child slowly takes his first steps. Stumbling his way to me. I am overwhelmed with pride.

- First words:
  I'm in my child's room, folding clothes. My child is in his crib. I walk to put his cloths in the closet, only to hear a little voice say "Mommy." I stop in the middle of my tracks. I look to see a little cute, cubby, brown skin baby smiling at me.
  "What?" I say faintly.
  "Mommy," my child says again, smiling and pointing at me.
  "Yes," I say smiling, "Mommy." I pick my child up and give him a kiss. "That's mommy's baby." I am filled with joy.

- First day of school:
  My son wears some khaki pants with a white polo shirt and black casual shoes. His hair is freshly cut and a Spiderman book bag is on his back. My son is nervous. He holds my hand tightly and looks up at me with fear in his eyes. I smile at him.
  "It's ok," I say, "don't be afraid. Mommy will be here at 3:00 to pick you up." I give him a hug and a kiss and watch him go inside his classroom. I can't believe how quickly he's grown. I am in disbelief.

- First game, recital, or performance:
  I sit in the bleachers and I watch as my son makes a three-pointer that wins the game. I jump up and down, cheering with the crowd. Happy about our victory. I am glad to be his mom.

- First crush:

I stand in the kitchen making dinner and my son comes up to me and asks me to help him make a Valentine's Day card for Alicia.
I smile at him. "Of course," I say. He is growing up. I am sad.

- First date:
  I wait nervously for my son to come back home from his date. I hope that he is safe. I look at the clock, 9: 55 p.m. Five minutes before curfew. A car pulls up. I hear footsteps, then a key jingling through the door. I rush to the door waiting for my son to walk through.
  "How did it go?" I say, trying to sound nonchalant.
  "Good," my son says.
  "Well, tell me about it." We sit in the kitchen and talk about how the date went. Inside, I am relieved.

- Prom:
  I wait at the bottom of the stairs for my child to come down. My son looks handsome in his black tuxedo and red silk tie. I take lots of pictures until he says "Mama, enough." I smile shyly and say I'm sorry. And my husband and I see them off. I am happy.

- High school graduation:
  I sit in the crowd and watch my son walk across the stage, receiving his diploma. He graduated with honors. I am proud.

These are so many things that I wished my mom could have experienced with me.

- **My first steps.** *I probably walked to the words "Come to daddy."*
- **My first words.** *It was probably daddy.*
- **My first day of school.** *I wore a navy blue skirt, a white button up shirt, and my hair was in pigtails.*
- **My first performance.** *Junior high, I cheered at basketball games.*
- **My first crush.** *Elementary school, some boy named Devon.*
- **My first date.** *A guy named Mark, he was my prom date. My brother came with me.*
- **My prom.** *I wore a cream halter top dress. It was short in the front and had a little train in the back. I wore gold, open-toed heels. My hair was in an updo.*
- **My high school graduation.** *I graduated with honors, Cum Laude.*

I don't want my child to experience this kind of pain. This void that is never filled. That is always aching. Always burning.

Although I am afraid of having children, it doesn't mean that I don't fantasize about being a Mom. It doesn't mean that I don't want to have those experiences that my mother missed. I do. I fantasize about having a child often. Seeing them smiling at me. Hearing them calling me "Mommy." I picture me taking them to the park. Pushing them on the swings. Sliding down the slide with them. Running around with them. But I also wonder how that day at the park will end.

- Will someone rob me?
- Will someone shoot up the park?
- Will a stray bullet hit me?

- Will the bullet hit me in the head?
- Will my child see?
- Will I die in front of my child?
- Will that child be a girl? (I fear having a girl)

So I have an on-going internal dilemma with myself…

I will live on through my child, but how will my child live on without me?

N

I want to be just like my mother. Family members and friends are convinced that my mother was an angel. They tell me all the time how sweet, kind, caring, and forgiving she was.

- Sisters didn't come to her baby shower.

Tues. July 26, 88
Time: 12:43 a.m.

My shower Sat. 23, 88 was awful. No one came, but 5 people Jimmie, Evelyn, Etta, Candy and Nette.

- Best friends slept with her boyfriend.

Saturday October 8, 1988

[My best friend] tells James everything I say so I guess you can call her James friend. I no longer say she's my friend ever.

- Boyfriend accused her of cheating.

*Fri. July 30, 88
Time: 10:28 a.m.*

James still accuses me of fooling around with [his best friend]. I hate his [best friend] more each day. He's the one who started this shit.

- Boyfriend cheated on her.

*May 9 Mon. 88
Time: 11:33 p.m.*

We were on the freeway and James discovered that [his baby mama] and her friends was following us. They drove up on the side of us and I looked right into the car. [James' baby mama] and her friends drove in front of us and then James discovered their car. He speeded up to catch them and they speeded up and got away.

This really made me upset, I mean what's going on? This really makes me wonder.

    No matter what anyone did, she was kind to them and she always forgave them.
    They say I act just like her. I laugh just like her. I talk just like her. I wonder what else I do like her. I strive to be like my mother. I want to be kind because that's how she was. I want to be caring because that's

how she was. I want to be understanding because that's how she was. I want to be just like her.

I love to write because my mother loved to write. This is something that we share. It seems like we are connected through this. But we are also connected through our bullet wounds. Her's in the middle of her head. Mine is in the middle of my stomach. Sometimes, while lying down in bed, I'll slowly run my fingers up and down my scar. I will see my mother. She'll lay down next me and smile. Then she'll slowly run her fingers up and down her scar. We'll stare at each other for awhile, both feeling our scars, both reminiscing about our death experiences. We are so much alike, but...

I just don't want to die like her...
    I just don't want to die like her...
        Lord, please don't let me die like her.

A Part of Me I Left Behind

"He's gone you know," she says in the back of my mind. I sit in my bedroom, gripping onto the bed, in my on-campus apartment not really sure if I'm having a psychotic breakdown or not. "Gone and never coming back."

And then a memory of him floods my mind. Him smiling down at me and calling me *"my little pooh bear."* I try to shake back the tears. I try not to break down. Not to end up in a state where I'm curling up in a ball hyperventilating with the thought of me losing my mind. So again I run. I go to places that are filled with people—the conference room in Lake Ontario where my *430 Advanced Fiction Workshop* class meets; the C-store on the GV's campus in Allendale; Buffalo Wild Wings with a friend; a student poetry slam. But it doesn't even matter because I'm still alone in my thoughts, no matter how crowded the place maybe.

The way my nine-year-old self looks at me makes me feel ashamed, with pigtails, eyes red from tears, and her skinny child-like figure, she's still grieving for our father—the way I left her, the way I've repressed her. I've lied to myself. Pretended I was fine and moved on while leaving her behind. But I never *really* left her, still there grieving over my father in some small ways.

"Do you understand what I'm saying," she says when I ignore her. "Daddy is gone and he isn't coming back." Another memory of him penetrates my mind without my permission—the sweet, sweet smell of his Christian Dior's Fahrenheit cologne and how it lingers when he leaves the room. I clutch at my chest.

"Stop!" I, my twenty-two-year-old self, plea. "Please stop!"

"You have to stop running Jana`." Another memory: his bright, perfect smile. I shake my head back and forth trying to shake out the memories of him.

"I can't, I can't do this," I say. And I can't. It's been thirteen years and I still can't think about the night I received the news about his death. It's been thirteen years since I've watched him get taken away in handcuffs, unaware that that would've been the last time I saw him alive—all because he was late for a court date. It's been thirteen years and I am still in denial, secretly hoping that one day he will show up to tell me that it's all been a cruel, cruel joke.

I can imagine him showing up at my apartment at Grand Valley smiling down at me with his perfect smile, his cologne filling up the room. I can hear his voice telling me that he's been away for a while and that he's sorry about all the important moments he's missed out on and that he's very proud of me. I can imagine all of this. Hope for it—I am still in denial.

"You can talk about Mama," my nine-year-old self says. "You can write and talk about her all day, but what about Daddy? Why can't you talk about him too?"

I don't answer because I know what she says is true. I can always talk about my mother; I'm strong enough for that. But my father—I can't talk about. The news of his death turned my whole world upside down and it has never been right since then. He was my protector, my love, my whole world.

"I'm not strong enough," I admit. "I'm not strong enough to talk about him." I tear up just thinking about it and my nine-year-old self sees this. She just shakes her head at me. And I feel ashamed. I have let her down. She's nine-years-old and can deal with the death of our father. But I, twenty-two-years-old, can't stomach the thought of his death.

"You're forgetting him you know," she tells me, adding salt to my wounds.

"I know," I admit weakly. Sometimes I forget what his voice sounded like or the way he laughed or the way he walked or sometimes, and just sometimes, the way he smelled.

"How can you forget about him?"

"I don't know," I whisper.

"You need to deal with this."

"I can't, I'm not strong enough."

"Daddy died of cancer, lymphoma," she begins to fire off.

"Stop."

"He was getting sicker and sicker while in a jail cell."

"Please,"

"You never got a chance to say goodbye, to say that you loved him."

"No more."

"He was all alone, no loved ones around."

I don't respond.

"He's gone Jana`!" I can no longer take what she's saying. So, I do what I do best…run. I go to the bathroom, my favorite place to cry—the only room that's *guaranteed* to have a lock on the door. I look at myself in the mirror, but I don't see me. I see her, my nine-year-old self that once innocent, sweet, happy face is now filled with, pain, anger, and anguish. There is a sense of maturity behind that four-feet-something-skinny-nine-year-old-figure.

"Remember how daddy used to chew on his tongue when he was concentrating hard on something?"

I feel stabs through my heart. I back away from the mirror. I can't run from her. I can't run from myself.

Nine years old and I see my father being handcuffed and taken away from downtown Detroit's 36th district courtroom. I cry into my auntie's chest. As if foreshadowing, part of me knows that this is the last time I will see him alive.

I back away from the mirror. My knees buckle. My balance is unstable. I can hardly catch my breath. I can't think about this. I'm not strong enough.

"Remember how Daddy used to stutter when he got upset?"

My auntie screams. She throws down the cordless phone, like it was scorching to the touch. Her piercing screams—over and over again. I recognize that scream. The scream of pain. The scream when something is wrong.

I back away from the mirror. My knees buckle. My balance is unstable. I can hardly catch my breath. I want to vomit. I can't take this anymore. I feel like I'm going to die. I just want her to stop. To stop making me remember; to stop causing me so much pain.

My auntie kneels down in the corner, weeping. I slowly walk up to her and ask her what's wrong. She looks up at me through tear-filled eyes.

"You poor, poor baby," she repeatedly says.

"You poor, poor baby," echoes through my head. I back away from the mirror. My knees buckle. My balance is unstable. I can hardly catch my breath. I want to vomit. I can't take this anymore. I slowly slide to the floor.

"Remember how he used to chase us with snot hanging from his nose? Remember how fun that used to be?"

"Please," I cry out, "please, no more."

"Your daddy's dead," my auntie finally says. "You lost your mother and now your daddy. You poor, poor baby." She begins to stroke my hair. Daddy is gone. I am alone.

A single tear falls from my eyes. I hug my auntie. Surprisingly enough, I'm hugging her to comfort her, I am numb.

And I've been numb ever since.

I start to cry out for him. "Daddy," I curl up in a ball. "Why did you leave me?"

"Remember when we were little and we used to sit on his lap?"

"Daddy," I say trying to catch my breath. "I miss you so much."

"Remember when he used to do our hair?"

"Daddy, why did you go?"

"Remember when he used to tell us that he loved us?"

"Please," I cry, "no more." But she doesn't stop. She keeps firing off memories that I try to forget. Like the times he yelled at the TV while watching basketball, football or boxing; the times he used to have all my male cousins downstairs in our basement boxing; the times he took my brother James and me to Omega's Coney

Island for breakfast every morning before school; the times he bit his tongue when he glided effortlessly around the skating ring; the times that he warned my brother and me about how it would be when he eventually died. Memories I avoid so I won't end up like I am now, curled up in a ball and hyperventilating.

"Daddy, please come back to me."

And then it happens. Just when everything is about to go black. Just when I straddle the line between a psychotic break and death, I see him. He's smiling down at me, but there's concern behind his beautiful brown eyes. He leans down over me and wraps me up in his muscular arms. I can smell Christian Dior's Fahrenheit cologne that he always wears.

"My little Nay-boo," he says rocking me back and forth while stroking my hair. "My silly little pooh bear, I *never* left."

The Great Adventure of Jana`Chantel's Death

Ladies and gentlemen! Boys and girls! Come! Come! Gather around and see this wonderful show! For it may thrill you. Or it may frighten you. It may freak you out. Or it may enlighten you. Behold, a girl that dies over and over again! Never in the same situation. Always in a different kind of way. So come, come, COME! Follow the line. Join the adventure. Because no matter what route you may take, this girl's fate always ends in the same way....

> The house I'm in is beautiful. Two stories and the room I'm in has two big picture windows. The weather outside is perfect, sunny without a cloud in the sky.
>
> I'm listening to music while my little nephew is beat-boxing along, while pretending to be driving. I look over at him and smile. I love his childhood innocence and I know that he will grow up to be someone great.
>
> It all happens so suddenly. The change of the weather comes from out of nowhere. The sirens go off as one, two, three, *four* tornadoes drop from out of the sky. My nephew and I don't have any time. We won't be able to make it down to the basement. I grab him and pull him to my chest as I grip on to the bed's head board.
>
> I can feel the power of the tornadoes as the storm runs through the house and lifts me into the sky. I wrap my arms tightly around my nephew as we begin to spin, spin higher through the air. Lord I just pray that *he* makes it out ok.

My auntie and I are driving down Newburgh Road, on our way to Wal-Mart. We're laughing and talking about our relationships in life. The sun is shining, and we let the windows down to let the cool breeze in.

My auntie turns over to me and laughs at the last thing I said, when a truck runs a red light and crashes into her side (the driver's side) of the car. Everything seems to be going fast. We do a complete turn and it's hard to make out any images. Our car finally comes to a stop when a car from behind us slams us into a nearby building.

All I can hear is my auntie's screams. High pitched and filled with fear and shock. I'm too struck with fear for anything to come out of my mouth. The car stops just over the broken windows that we had just crashed through. I look over at my auntie. She's ok, besides a few cuts and scrapes.

"Jana`," she whispers to me. She looks terrified. I look up to see a pole swing back and forth towards us. It's closer to my auntie and by the way that it's swinging it will hit her.

Without thinking I unfasten my seatbelt and jump in front of her as the pole rips through my body. My shirt becomes soaking wet and I know it's my blood. The pain is agonizing.

> It's the worst asthma attack I ever had, but the symptoms are all the same—the tightness in the chest, the difficulty breathing. My inhaler isn't working. And I can't calm myself down enough to dial my aunt or 911. I begin to feel lightheaded and now I am barely breathing. My cell phone slips out my hand. I fall to the floor. I never catch my next breathe.

23

My cousin Javon and I are on our way to a doughnut shop to meet up with a guy that he talked to from an internet ad website. The guy is interested in a phone that my cousin is selling. I'm a bit uneasy as I ride along with him. People are so shady nowadays that I'm nervous that the guy will try to rob my cousin for the phone. But I don't say anything. I just ride along silently with him.

We pull up into the doughnut shop's parking lot to see the guy and his friend are already there, waiting outside the doughnut shop's door. They're Arabic or maybe Chaldean, I don't know. Javon gets out of the car. I stay in the car as I watch Javon approach them. He pulls out the iPhone and hands it to them to look at. They inspect it, trying to find out if the phone has any scratches or nicks on it. They are satisfied with what they see.

Just as I expected, the guy pulls a gun out on my cousin. I jump out the car.

"No!" I scream, "Javon!" The guy's friend looks over at me and smirks as he pulls out a gun and fires it at me. The fire enters my chest, and I collapse on the ground. Blood pours out of me and I can hear Javon yelling my name.

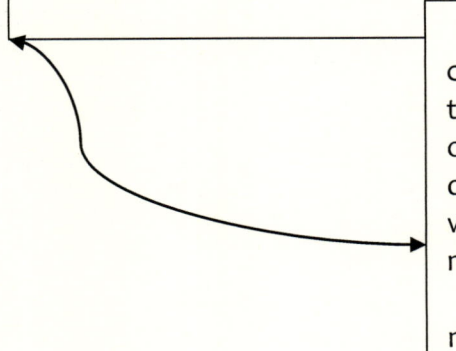

I lay on the beige leather couch in my auntie's living room trying to fall asleep. The neighbors outside are blasting music. I take a deep breath and close my eyes while I think of things that will make me fall asleep.

Gunshots go off outside. I never get the chance to open my eyes. A stray bullet goes through the patio window and strikes me in the head. I am finally able to sleep.

24

The house is on fire. I'm not sure why I am here, but I am. I came to visit a lady that I don't even know and I see that her house is on fire.

"Help me!" she yells as she sees me, "Please help me, my son is still inside." The look on her face is heartbreaking, filled with anguish and pain. I quickly run inside. The smoke is thick and I begin to choke. I call out her son's name as I continue to search through the house.

I find him hiding in the back of his mother's closet. I pick him up and head back to the front door. We almost make it when the ceiling collapses in front of us. I manage to get him through an opening, but the way is too small for me. He looks back once he reaches the door.

"Go!" I say through coughs, "go to your mom." With one last look he goes. The fire continues to blaze uncontrollably. I run back to the closet where he was hiding and I close the door. I lie down and curl up in a ball on the closet floor. I close my eyes and wait for the fire to take me.

See Jana's Dreams!

Ladies and gentlemen! Boys and girls! Calm! Calm! Calm yourselves down please! There's no need to be upset!

"What kind of *freak* show is this?!"
"What kind of person is this?!"
"She's a freak!"
"She's crazy!"
"She isn't normal!"

I hear the people's responses to my dreams. I look out of the box that I'm kept in and I see all of my spectators. They all look shocked, scared, amazed, or intrigued. But disbelief is the dominant reaction. I look so normal sitting here on a stool in my glass box.

"You'd never think that a person like her would be thinking of something like *that*."
"She *looks* normal."
"Mommy, I'm scared."

Ladies and gentlemen! Boys and girls! Please! Please! Please settle down! Come! Come! Come! Let us see what else this young woman thinks!

I GET CANCER

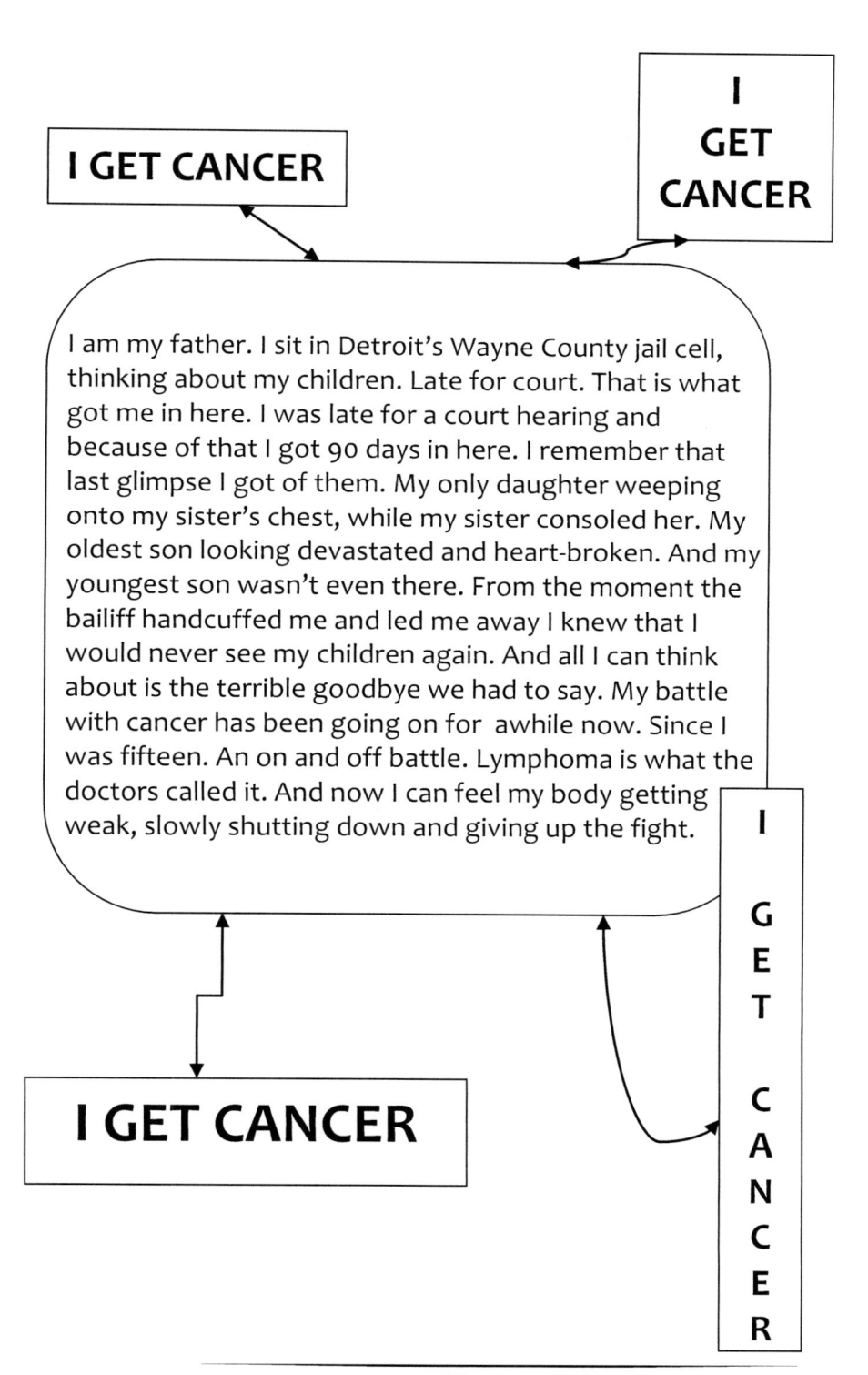

I GET CANCER

I am my father. I sit in Detroit's Wayne County jail cell, thinking about my children. Late for court. That is what got me in here. I was late for a court hearing and because of that I got 90 days in here. I remember that last glimpse I got of them. My only daughter weeping onto my sister's chest, while my sister consoled her. My oldest son looking devastated and heart-broken. And my youngest son wasn't even there. From the moment the bailiff handcuffed me and led me away I knew that I would never see my children again. And all I can think about is the terrible goodbye we had to say. My battle with cancer has been going on for awhile now. Since I was fifteen. An on and off battle. Lymphoma is what the doctors called it. And now I can feel my body getting weak, slowly shutting down and giving up the fight.

I GET CANCER

I GET CANCER

A serial killer is on the loose and I am at home by myself. My auntie and my little sister are away. It's getting late and I am getting tired. I put on my pjs and I go to my auntie's bedroom, lock the door and go to bed.

I am awakened by a noise. I sit up in bed. I believe I just heard the front door open. I slowly and quietly walk to the bedroom door. My hand rests on the door knob. I hear the front door close. I open the door to see if it is my auntie. I am mistaken.

I see a person standing in the middle of the hallway. I can't tell if the person is a man or a woman because they are wearing a ski mask. My heart begins to race. I try to close and lock the bedroom door, but the person is quicker.

They pull me by my hair and drag me into the hallway. I struggle against them but they are too strong. They stab me in the chest. My screams are muffled by their hand.

They stab me again in the stomach. The pain is agonizing and I'm praying to God that this person will stop. They stab me again in the stomach. My body becomes limp in my killer's arms. They release me and I fall to the floor. Blood pour onto the carpet. And the last thing I see is my killer's feet walking back out the front door.

> I lay down to sleep. I dream of seeing my parent's again. They look at me and smile. My mother steps towards me and hugs me. "Welcome home, sweetie," she says. My dad continues to smile at me. I never wake from my dream.

I'm standing on the rooftop looking down at the cars that are more the ten stories below me. All I can keep thinking about is the last thing he said to me, "We should just be friends."

I feel a rip through my heart. My stomach begins to jerk as tears fall from my eyes. Good girls always get overlooked. I'm not used to having a broken heart. The pain is unbearable.

He's not ready to commit to me. He still wants to mess around with other girls. What do they have that I don't? Why can't he be happy and satisfied with me?

I step up on the roof's edge. I take a deep breath. I spread my arms, arch my back, and rise up on my tiptoes. I slowly lean forward and close my eyes. I feel the wind against my face.

ENTER HER MIND!!

It's storming outside. Thunder and lightning rip through the sky. The tree outside my little sister's room is rocking back and forth. I stare at it in a daze. Watching the beauty and yet the dangers of Mother Nature. The rain is pouring. The wind is at full speed. And this big oak tree is rocking as if the wind was providing it a beat. I'm uneasy about it. And then the grand finale, lighting strikes the tree and the tree leans closer to the apartment. The wind continues to blow strong.

"Enough!" one of the spectators yell. "Enough! I can't take it anymore! It's just too much death!"

"I'm getting out of here!"

"Where's the exit?!"

Ladies and gentlemen! Boys and girls! There is nowhere! Nowhere! Nowhere else you can run! You will always be thinking about her! You will always be thinking about her and her obsession with death! So please! Please! Please stay! And let us continue to see the other ways that she dies!

A lady gets up and slowly walks over to the glass box that I am sitting in. She looks me over intensely, as if trying to find some kind of physical deformity. She is dissatisfied when she finds I'm normal. It just makes her angrier. Her thin, brown eyebrows pushed together; her thin, red lipsticked mouth pursed together; her gloved, thin hands clutching her handbag. She glares.

"She deserves to be in the circus!" she turns around to the rest of the spectators. "I'm leaving! Come on Jimmy!" She grabs her son and leaves where she believes the exit is. The maestro is unfazed by her departure.

Ladies and gentlemen! Boys and girls! Let us! Let us! Let us continue our journey through her dreams!

I Get Shot

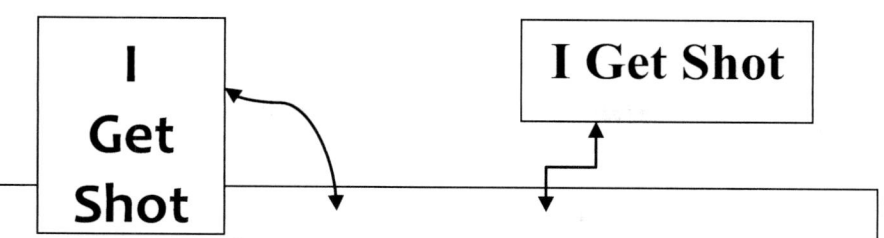

I Get Shot

I am my mother. I am in the house on St. Mary's street. I walk around the house, attending to things. Washing dishes. Sweeping and moping the floors. Folding clothes. My daughter, Jana`, sits on the floor watching me.
There's a knock at the front door. I walk to the front door.
"Who is it?" I say.
"Hey, Gwen it's..." I don't catch his name.
"James isn't here," I tell him.
"I know, he told me I could come over here and get something," he says.

I open the door, expecting a friendly welcome, but instead I get rushed by three men in baseball caps. I feel the excruciating pain of their punches and kicks.

"Take us to the safe!" They punch me in my mouth. "Take us to the damn safe!" They yell punching and hitting me along the way. The pain of their hits is unbearable and I begin to scream. Jana` begins to scream.

"Give us the money!" they demand. I give them the contents in the safe.

They drag me to the basement and my daughter's screams become louder. I'm dragged down the basement stairs. My heart races. I know I won't be walking back up those stairs. The men push me up on the wall. One of them puts a pillow over my head. Reacting instinctively I put my hands over my face.
I hear a gun fire off. I hear them walk back upstairs. Shortly after, I hear my daughter fall down the stairs.

I look over at her in a daze. I see that she is covered in blood. I realize that it is my blood that she is drenched in. She's screaming, as if she knows what happened. Her screams begins to fade. I hope her father gets here in time.

I am at a wedding. I am at a funeral. I honestly do not know what occasion I am at, but it is an occasion that allows all of my family and friends to gather together. We are on the eastside of Detroit. Farewell's recreation field to be exact. My brother, James, and I walk to the ceremony laughing and talking. The weather is fine, but I have a weird feeling about it.

"Come on Jana`, we're about to be late!" my brother says suddenly. We rush to the event. I look up at the sky and then it happens. Lighting strikes everywhere. Tornadoes form out of the sky. Rain and hail pours down. It is Armageddon. Everyone screams and tries to run for some kind of cover.

"Jana`! Come on! Come on!" James screams. He and I run towards the recreation building. Lighting strikes close by us, tornadoes swirl closer to us. James and I keep running. Running to stay alive. We get closer, but lighting strikes again. This time hitting me. I scream in agony. My body shakes as the electricity rips through my body. I am on fire.

> I live to see eighty. I've had a good career, beautiful children, and a wonderful marriage. My husband lies next to me in bed. I tell him goodnight and give him a kiss. I sigh, cut off the light next to our bed, and drift off to sleep.

Life is starting to become unbearable. It's just one big disappointment after another. I go out for a walk so I can let off some steam and clear my head. All I can feel is emotional pain. And I can't seem to find the silver lining that in the past, I'm *always* able to find. I feel like I just want to die.

I come to a main street and traffic is moving. Without thinking, being driven by emotion, I continue towards the street. A city bus honks its horn and tries to brake. Headlights. Headlights. Headlights.

SHE IS OBSESSED WITH DEATH

THIS IS NOT A DREAM!!!

THIS IS REALITY!!!

This is not a dream! I am in the house on Bloom. I stand in the living room behind the couch. I stand in the living room behind the couch and in front of the wall that separates the living room from the kitchen. I stand there laughing. I look from my friend to my brother. And then I see fire. And then I feel something rip through my body. And then I feel a burning, vibrational feeling. It was the gun, it was the gun. The gun just went off. I kick and scream in agonizing pain. I am about to die. I am about to die. I just got shot. I can't feel my leg. And I am about to die.

This is not a dream! This is not a dream! This is a nightmare!

"I can't take anymore of this!!!!!"

This is reality!
    I am about to die.
        Come back.
            Come back.

"Where is the exit?!"

"FOR GOD'S SAKE I JUST WANT TO GET OUT OF HERE!!!"

THIS IS NOT A DREAM!!!

"For God's sake I just want to get out of here!" the lady screams. She's been trying to get out of here for awhile now, but no matter where she goes she is still able to see my death. The other spectators are speechless. It is as if the life has been sucked out of them.

The maestro looks at the crowd pleased. He had just shown them my vivid dreams and dark thoughts, and he knows that someone who is this obsessed with death isn't normal. There's not a day that goes by when the thought of death doesn't cross my mind. I can't help it. It's something that's beyond my control.

"Can you let us go now?!" the lady screams.

"I want to go home!" another yells.

"We shouldn't have come here!"

"She needs to be in an insane asylum!" These are things that I haven't heard before or thought before.

"I don't get it mommy," a little boy says, "you told me, when my goldfish died, that death was a part of life—why is *she* a freak because she thinks about it?" I open my eyes. No one answers his question. I smile at him… ⟶ THE END

Because They Said That Good Things Will Come To Those Who Wait

All it takes is a fifteen minute phone call for my heart to race, for the stomach butterflies to flutter, and sometimes, for my asthma to act up.

My phone rings at certain times of the day [4:00, 6:00, and 10:15 p.m.] and I look at the caller ID to see the word *Private*. *Private*. The word is ironic, since I already know who's calling.

"Hello, you have a prepaid/debt call from [pause] 'Mr. Beautiful Smile [1]'" I love hearing that name after the woman's automated voice. "To accept this prepaid/debit call press 0, [press 0]. This call is subject to be monitored. Thank-you for using Embarq."

"Hello," he always says.

"Hey," I always say.

"Wasup Jana`, what you doing?"

"Nothing, just [insert: reading, studying, or watching TV]."

A fifteen minute phone call, that's all it takes for me to be on cloud nine. For me to experience a high

---

[1] For personal reasons, let's just call him Mr. Beautiful Smile

without *actually* taking drugs, just a fifteen-minute phone call.

I never care what we talk about, just as long as I hear his voice. I picture his face while he talks. His flawless light brown skin, his freshly cut hair shows off the waves that run through it, his goatee neatly lined up. I see his smile as he laughs—his straight, pearly white teeth. That smile, that beautiful smile that causes me to smile.

"So, wasup with you?" he says.

"Noth..."

"This call is from the Michigan Department of Corrections." The woman's automated voice always interrupts.

I hate when she does that because it reminds me of our situation—taking me away from my high—and, less importantly, it causes us to repeat whatever we had just said.

We usually talk about what it's going to be like when he comes home, or we reminisce about how it was when he was home.

"You gonna be on yo way back to school when I come home. I ain't gonna like that," he says sometimes when we were talking about our future. Or:

"I remember when I first moved to Rudgate," when we were talking about our past.

"You have one minute left," the automated woman always says, bringing us back to the present.

"Well, I was just calling to see what you was doing," he will sometimes say. "I love you and I'll talk to you later."

"I love you too," I will always say, sadly. I never want to get off the phone with him. The feeling of loneliness overwhelms me. I go back to writing papers, reading books, studying for tests, and sleeping alone. All the while wishing he is here with me, talking to me as I write my papers, lying in my arms as I read Shakespeare to him, quizzing me for an upcoming test, and holding me in his arms as we sleep through the night together.

"Bye-bye."

"Thank-you for using Embarq." The automated woman says again. Man, I hate that lady.

■■■

Junior Year of High School:

"I'm so tired of everybody talking about *Mr. Beautiful Smile*," my friend L.J. tells me as we sit on my front porch. I stare off at the sky, frowning up at the sun.

"Who is this *Mr. Beautiful Smile* person?" I ask, frowning at the name. I've been hearing a lot about him. My cousin became friends with him. I keep wondering, what kind of name is *Mr. Beautiful Smile*?

"He just moved in Rudgate," she says. I didn't know. I spent the whole summer away at my cousin's house. "He came to my house with Mike on my birthday. It was the first time I met him and I got into it with him."

I just smile at her. I can tell that she is annoyed by him, which makes me wonder if she likes him.

"He thinks he's the [censored]," she finally says. I nod. I know that I will have to meet him for myself to form an opinion of him.

**

I finally meet him on the first day of school. He walks on the bus with his sisters. I see L.J. roll her eyes when she sees him. I smile. His demeanor is strong. Confident. Very sure of himself. He walks down the aisle as if he knows that "he's the man." A smile is on his face.

I see something there. Something that I can't put my finger on...yet.

■■■

"Step through the metal detector please," a lady correctional officer says. The detector beeps. She looks me up and down.

"Hmmm," she says studying me. "Take off those boots. Sometimes boots that have the buckles on them cause the machine to go off." I unzip my boots. I look up to see her smiling at me.

"You would've had to take them off anyways," she says as-a-matter-of-factly. "Ok, step back through," she says once I have my boots off. The detector is silent.

"Ok, turn around and hold out your arms." I turn around and hold out my arms. The lady correctional officer pats me down.

"Put your hands in your back pockets." I put my hands in my back pockets.

"Turn around and pull out your front pockets." I turn around and pull out my front pockets.

"Open your mouth please." I open my mouth, feeling awkward. She smiles with a look that says, "I'm-just-doing-my-job."

"Turn your boots upside down and shake them please." I turn my boots upside down and shake them.

"Ok, take off your socks and show me the bottoms of your feet." I slowly take off my socks and show her the bottoms of my feet.

"Ok, put everything back on." I put everything back on, happy for the search to end.

I show my ID to some more correctional officers, and they give me a visitor's badge. The lady correctional officer leads me to the visitor's room. It's been two-and-a-half years since he's been locked up. It's been two-

and-a-half years since I've seen him. No car, so we only communicate by letters and phone. It's hard for me to get these butterflies in my stomach to calm down.

∙∙∙

Junior Year of High School:

> *Phone Rings.*
> "Hello." I say, answering the phone.
> "Hello, can I speak to Doug?" I recognize the voice as *Mr. Beautiful Smile's*. I just spent time hearing that voice mess with me on the school bus.
> "He's not here," I say about my cousin who's a year older than me, "he's at football practice."
> "Is this little ugly?" he says. He's been calling me that on the bus. I picture his sixteen-year-old self smiling.
> "No." I say. [Pause] "Why are you being mean to me?"
> "I'm just [censored] with you."
> "Oh, ok" I say, glad to no longer be picked on.
> "Ah, have you ever liked any of Doug's friends?" he asks.
> "No."
> "Why not?"
> "I don't know. Just haven't liked any of them," I say, confused as to where this conversation is going.
> "Would you ever mess with any of Doug's friends?" he asks. I'm caught off guard by that question.
> "I don't know," I say. "I guess if I really liked them."
> "Would you ever mess with me?" I'm *really* caught off guard by *that* question. I just found out who he was today. Yet strangely, a part of me wants to say yes to his question. What is it about him that's attracting

me? It's not his good looks, his popularity, or the way he has with girls. But, as I look back at it now, five years later, I can say that it was that glimpse of goodness that attracted me to him.

"I don't know," I say hesitantly. "Maybe."

"Oh," he says, "Well, just tell Doug I called."

"Ok." I hang up the phone and stare at it for a while. Something tells me that he *really* didn't call for my cousin Doug. I stare at the phone thinking about *Mr. Beautiful Smile.*

• •

The visiting room looks grim. Dingy, white walls. Blue cushions on hard metal-like chairs. A security desk sits in a corner in front of the room. Numerous vending machines. Microwaves at the back on a counter. A book shelf along the back wall. A toy area stationed at the back corner. The bright toys can't change the mood of this room. But three beautiful black-and-white photographs hang above the vending machines. A piece of art work. And, along with them is *Mr. Beautiful Smile.*

He stands up from his chair once he sees me. He looks good, just like I remembered. He still has that beautiful smile. He still has that pretty light brown skin. We hug for the first time in what seems like forever. The lady correctional officer stands by us. I feel her presence as we kiss. She's just like that automated woman on the phone, always there to keep me aware of our situation.

He leads me to a sitting area, and I look at him closely for the first time. His hair is nicely cut, and I can see waves throughout his head. He always had a thing for looking good. I see a tattoo on the right side of his neck that wasn't there before. It's a red star (his favorite color) that has his name going through it. A star, I wonder if that is predicting his future.

"What made you want to fuck with me?" he asks me after awhile. He's asked me this question a couple of times.

"You don't see what I see." I say. This is true. I don't think anyone sees what I see. I guess that's one of the side effects to being creative. A painter can look at a blank canvas and see a beautiful portrait. A sculptor can look at a slab of marble and see a masterpiece. I look at *Mr. Beautiful Smile* and see a great man. A man who is so loving and caring. A man you can depend on and who will always be there for you. A man who in the end will always make the right decision (no matter how long it takes him to get there). A man who can be admired.

"You got a lot of potential," I finally say, looking at him.

He smiles. "Yeah," he says. We both sit silent for a minute—holding each other's hands.

■■

Junior Year of High School:

"I never kissed a boy," I say to L.J., our friend Mike, and *Mr. Beautiful Smile* as we wait for the bus home.

"You never kissed a boy?" L.J. asks, laughing. "You poor baby."

I smile shyly. I see *Mr. Beautiful Smile* looking at me smiling.

"You never kissed a boy?" he asks. I shake my head as I look down at the ground. I'm embarrassed. "You lying."

"No, I'm not," I say still looking at the ground.

"I don't know, how Doug and yo brother is, you probably haven't." I look up to see him looking at me. I wonder what he's thinking. Maybe he's thinking that it's cute that I haven't kissed a boy. Or maybe he's thinking that it's sad that I haven't kissed a boy. Or maybe, just maybe, he's thinking about kissing me.

I ride the bus home, lost in my own world—thinking about homework, upcoming test, and of course *Mr. Beautiful Smile*. I finally get off at my stop only to see that *Mr. Beautiful Smile* is getting off too. We walk home together.

"I don't know if you noticed," he says as we're walking, "but I like you."

I look down at the ground, trying not to smile. "Oh," I finally say. I am surprised by this confession, but secretly happy inside.

"Usually girls are able to tell when a guy likes them."

"I can't," I say. I'm not like other girls. I'm too preoccupied with my studies to notice when a guy is flirting with me.

Now that I think about it, five years later, I wonder if I told him that I liked him too. But what I do remember is this:

I walked into my house, thinking about *Mr. Beautiful Smile*.

■■

End of Freshmen Year of College:

My cell phone rings.
"Hello," I say answering my phone.
"Oh, you sound like you was sleep," Doug says.
"Let me talk to her," I hear *Mr. Beautiful Smile* say in the background.
"Nah, she sound like she was sleep," Doug says to him.

"No, I'm not," I say objecting. Doug does not like the fact that his friend, *Mr. Beautiful Smile,* is "talking" to me, his cousin (who is more like a sister to him). It might be his over protectiveness, or the fact that he knows how *Mr. Beautiful Smile* is with girls, but whatever the case, Doug doesn't like it. I hear Doug hand him the phone.

"Hello," *Mr. Beautiful Smile* says into the phone.

"Hey," I say.

"You don't sound like you was sleep. I'm 'bout to come up there to chill with you."

"Ok." I wait for him to walk from Doug's room to the family room where I sit on the couch. He walks in smiling.

"Hey," he says.

"Hey," he walks over and sits next to me on the couch. We sit in the dark, just looking at the TV. I move closer to him. Run my hand through his head, feeling his waves. I touch his right hand. It pains me to know that we are nothing more than just friends.

"Did you ask Doug if I talk to other girls?" he asks me as time moves on.

"Yeah," I say.

"Why didn't you just ask me?"

"I don't know," I say looking at the TV. "Do you?"

"Yeah, I do."

My heart sinks. He's the *only* guy I'm talking to. I nod, trying hard not show that I'm a little hurt.

"How do you feel about me?" I ask.

He smiles a little and turns his head. "I mean, I like you a lot." He says turning back towards me. "But I'm just not looking for a girlfriend right now."

Not the answer that I want. I like him more than he likes me. My feelings for him are stronger, much stronger. I barely sleep because he's always on my mind. My stomach is always in knots when I hear his name, or see him. I start to realize that I am falling in love with him.

He yawns and stretches. "I'm tired, I'm about to go to bed."

"No, stay." I don't want him to go. I like having him around me.

He smiles. "Nah, I better go to bed." He gets up. I feel a part of me leaving with him. We don't spend much time with each other; he's always hanging out with Doug. But when we do spend time with each other, I cherish each moment.

**

August 9, 2007:

Mr. Beautiful Smile gets locked up for attempting to sell drugs.

I don't know who told me or how I found out, but I do remember this:

I write *Mr. Beautiful Smile* a letter telling how I feel about him. I tell him that I love him. I tell him that I will be there for him. I tell him that I will wait for him. Because it doesn't matter that he committed a crime. And it doesn't matter that we aren't able to be together at this time. All that matters is that I love him.

2007-2010

Things they say:

"You're talking to one of Doug's friends?" a cousin says. "Girl, you don't need to be talking to him, all of Doug's friends is nothing but a bunch of wanna-be thugs."

"He locked up?!" a younger cousin says. "What he do?!"

"You gonna wait for him?" my uncle's girlfriend says with an eyebrow raised.

"Girl, you a good one," a friend says.

"I don't think I could wait for my man if he got locked up," a girl says.

"You're young," my auntie tells me. "You should be going out on dates, out to eat, out to the movies. You shouldn't be putting *your life* on hold boo."

"You should have niggas you talk to on the side," a male cousin says. "You young, man, you need to be out here getting niggas fo' they money."

"He's just trying to lock you down right along with him," another cousin says. "That's not fair to you. What can he do for you?"

"What if he gets out and cheats on you?" my auntie asks me.

Things I say or think:

"You don't know him. He's not a thug."
"He just made a bad decision."
"Yeah, I'm going to wait for him."
"Yeah."
I just nod.
"I'm not putting my life on hold."
"I don't want to talk to nobody but *Mr. Beautiful Smile*. And besides, I'm not like that." I can't imagine talking to anyone just for their money.
"Nobody's locking me down. I *choose* to wait for him. And it's not all about what he can do for me."

"It's a risk I'm willing to take, but no matter what, I won't regret my decision."

■■■

No one sees what I see. Sometimes I get frustrated. Most of the times I just don't care. He has so many good qualities:
    1.   He's sweet:

He sends me a card, for no reason. The front of the card has a brown teddy bear hugging a heart. And sticking out in front of that is a rose and another heart, intertwined together by a ribbon.
The front of the card reads:
"Dreaming of You"
The inside reads:
"When I dream of you I see someone who I feel so lucky to love. Someone who inspires me, makes me laugh, and loves me for who I am. But most of all, someone who makes me so happy—the one I love with all my Heart. Love, Mr. Beautiful Smile. Thinking of you."

    2.   He's caring:

"I didn't like for you to see me with other girls," he says to me on our last visit.
"Why?" I ask.
"Because I didn't," he says smiling. "Doug and I would pull up to yo house with some girls and I'd be like 'Man, there go Jana`.'"
I laugh.
He smiles and looks away "That's how I knew that I really cared for you," he turns back to me, looking me straight in the eyes.

3. He's loyal:

"There is this girl who writes me, who I think likes me," he says to me on our first visit. "So I try not to talk to her too much."
"Why?" I ask, looking down at the floor.
"Because she ain't worth [censored] things up with you."
I look up to see him looking at me. I smile.

4. He's respectful (especially to me):

"It took us this long to get to where we're at now," he says on our last visit. We were talking about our relationship.
"Five years," I say, giving an exact time period.
"Yeah," he says smiling, "I was taking my time with you." He leans back in his chair and folds his hands. "I was being a gentleman."
I smile. "I know that's what I like about you."
"Yeah," he says, leaning forward. He extends his right hand out to me. I take his hand, giving him a light-hearted handshake.
We both laugh.

5. He's honest:

"Jana` you deserve the best guy out here," he writes in a letter, "I'm not saying I can't be the guy eventually, but right now I got [censored] I gotta deal with. So I'm not going to take advantage of your feelings you have for me, now that I know how you feel about me. I'd rather we break now so we can have an honest and meaningful relationship later."

6. He looks out for others:

"I need to come home so I can help take care of my mama," he says to me on the phone. *"She needs my help."*

7. He's unselfish:

"This guy I'm cool with owed somebody some money," he says on one of our visits. *"So I gave him the money to pay them back."*
"That was nice of you," I say as I look down at our hands intertwined together.
"Yeah, if I can help someone else out then I will."

8. He's always willing to protect his self and those he loves:

"I don't like my little sister's boyfriend," he says on a visit.
"Why?" I don't understand what he has against him.
He shakes his head. *"He seems like the controlling type, I don't like that."*

9. I just love him.:

There are times that I'm not really sure as to why I love him. I just know that I love him, and for me that is enough. And for me he is worth the wait.

**

Each one of these qualities is like a brush stroke to that beautiful portrait, a chip into that masterful sculpture. Slowly but surely, the masterpiece of *Mr. Beautiful Smile* will be revealed to the rest of the world.

The things he says or writes:

"I want to go to school when I get home."
"I don't want to go back to Inkster. If I go back over there, I'll hang around the same crowd again and I'll be tempted to sell drugs."
"Over the past 5-6 months I've been realizing one way or another that some things I do and some of my ways of thinking need to change for the better before I come home."
"Will you help me apply for school and financial aid?"
"I don't want to get back in trouble."
"I don't want to get back in trouble."

The things I say or think:

"That's good. What do you want to go to school for?"
"Well, we'll just have to keep you away from there."
"That's good that you're seeing that."
"Of course I will."
"I won't let you."
"I won't let you."

■■

They say that good things will come to those who wait. Right now I am waiting. I wait to hear from *Mr. Beautiful Smile* by letter. I wait to hear from him by phone. I wait to see him again. I wait for him to come home—slowly crossing the days off of the calendar as they go by. *Only a few months left. May. June. July.*

I don't mind waiting because I know that he'll be worth it. A masterpiece takes time to create and once it is done, it is much more appreciated. *Mr. Beautiful Smile* is my Michelangelo's David—a beautiful piece of art that inspires me.

So my phone will sometimes ring and *Private* will show up on my caller ID. My heart will race, the stomach butterflies will flutter, and my asthma will sometimes act up. I will answer the phone to hear:

"Hello you have a prepaid/debt call from [pause] *'Mr. Beautiful Smile.'* To accept this prepaid/debit call press 0, [press 0]. This call is subject to be monitored. Thank-you for using Embarq."

Still Waiting For Good Things To Come

January 8, 2011:

I lay on my cousin's brown, suede couch crying—the soft cushion rest gently on my cheek. My stomach jerks, my chest heaves, and I try to catch my breath as tears stream down my face. My heart is broken. Nothing is the way I thought it would be.

This time there is no waiting on letters, no checking the mailbox to see if he has written me yet. There is no waiting for phone calls, no answering the phone and hearing that awful automated woman's voice, *"Hello, you have a prepaid/debt call from [pause] 'Mr. Beautiful Smile.' To accept this prepaid/debit call press 0, [press 0]. This call is subject to be monitored. Thank-you for using Embarq."* And this time there are no visits, no more taking off my shoes, emptying out my pockets and lifting up my tongue. This time it is different.

It should be better...but it's not.

———

Friday July 9, 2010 (29 days until *Mr. Beautiful Smile* comes home):

My cell phone rings.

Private. Appears on my caller ID.

"Hello, you have a prepaid/debt call from [pause] '*Mr. Beautiful Smile*,'" the automated woman greets me. "To accept this prepaid/debt call press 0, [press 0]. This call is subject to be monitored. Thank-you for using Embarq."

"Hey," I say with a smile on my face. He will be coming home pretty soon.

"Wasup Jana`, what you doing?"

"Nothing, just at my cousin Noland's house."

"Oh yeah, it's about time you got out the house."

I get up to go outside for some more privacy. "Yeah," I say sitting down on the back steps of my cousin's apartment building.

He sighs. "I'm worried about how it's going to be when I come home."

"Why?"

"Doug and them are throwing me a party when I get home. I know that girls are going to be trying to talk to me."

"I trust you."

He sighs again. "I just don't want to [censored] things up with you."

"I trust you *Mr. Beautiful Smile*." Fear builds up in my chest. *Mr. Beautiful Smile* has been talking like this for days now.

"I just know how I am. I'm going…"

"This call is from the Michigan Department of Corrections," the woman's automated voice interrupts.

"I'm going to want some space." he continues.

"So what? You don't want us to be together when you get home?" The fear intensifies. I can see it already: the endless amount of girls he'll be messing with, the absent phone calls, the endless nights of me crying. But I shake it off.

"No it's not that. I'm just not sure if you're going to be able to handle it."

"I mean," I get up and walk a little to calm the nerves. "I can understand that. I'll be able to handle it." In reality, I don't. I just don't want him to leave.

"And you'll trust me?"

"Yeah, why wouldn't I?"

He sighs yet again. "Alright."

"You have one minute left." This time I am glad that she signals the end of this conversation.

"I'll call you later."

"Ok."

"I love you."

"I love you too."

"Bye Bye."

Mr. Beautiful Smile never does call me back.

January 8, 2011:

"I'm just not ready to be in a relationship."

"I'm just not ready to be in a relationship," I keep hearing his voice say to me. I just don't understand what I did wrong. Why am I not enough for him? Why doesn't he want to be with me?

Again my stomach jerks, again my chest heaves, and again I try to catch my breath as tears stream down my face. My heart is broken. I wrap my arms around myself, and I curl up into a ball, wishing that my father was here to comfort me. To tell me that everything will be ok as he strokes my hair.

Why am I not enough for *Mr. Beautiful Smile*?

Why am I not enough for him?

Sunday July, 11 2010 (27 days until *Mr. Beautiful Smile* comes home):

    I haven't spoken to *Mr. Beautiful Smile* since Friday. And to be honest, I've been worried ever since. I think that *Mr. Beautiful Smile* no longer wants to be with me when he gets out. He wants to be free. He wants to do what he wants to do. Talk to whoever he wants to. Have sex with anyone.
    He doesn't want to be with me.
    I lay in my bed thinking. The late 5 p.m. sun shining through the bedroom blinds. I sigh. I've been having daydreams about *Mr. Beautiful Smile* telling me that he no longer wants to be in a relationship with me when he gets home. That he wants to be single and mess with other girls. My heart hurts just thinking about that.
    My cell phone rings.
    Private.
    My worst fears get confirmed. *Mr. Beautiful Smile* reads me a letter that he has written. I can't remember it from detail to detail, but the gist of it was this:

- He tells me that we shouldn't be together when he comes home.
- I shouldn't let him be my first
- He knows that he will be having sex with other girls.

    "I want to do you right," he says. "I want to take you out on dates and stuff like that. Will you let me do that?"

"Yeah," my voice cracks a little. He doesn't say anything. He just listens to me cry. And I cry hard. Feeling like my whole world is crashing down.

He sighs. "Just please don't get you a boyfriend." As if the thought of me being with someone else will kill him.

"I don't want to be with anyone but you." But he doesn't feel the same. And I won't be the only one he talks to.

January 8, 2011:

"Come on Jana`, pull yourself together," I say wiping away my tears, only for a fresh batch to take its place. "You will get through this. It will get better, I promise." But at this moment it isn't getting better. There's a pain that I have never felt before. A pain that is foreign to me. A pain of a heart breaking. A pain of realizing that your first love doesn't feel the same way about you.

"Just calm down Jana`," I hold myself tight. "Everything's going to be ok."

I remember what I said a long time ago when people advised me that I shouldn't mess with *Mr. Beautiful Smile* in the first place, "No matter what, I won't regret my decision."

"I won't regret my decision."

"I won't regret my decision."

September 10, 2010:

Mr. Beautiful Smile is released today and I still haven't heard from him. I've been waiting all day for him to call, wanting to hear his voice without that automated woman's voice, but I don't get anything. I thought that he would at least call to let me know that he made it out ok, to say that he's happy or anything, but nothing. I keep telling myself over and over again to be patient. That he will call me eventually. But still, nothing.

I break down and call my cousin Doug.
"Hello."
"Hey Doug, is *Mr. Beautiful Smile* with you?"
"Oh yeah, he talking to his probation officer right now. You want me to tell him to call you when he gets out?"
"Yeah."
"Alright."

I try to occupy myself by reading, doing some homework, and watching TV. None of these things help. I keep waiting for my phone to ring and for it to be *Mr. Beautiful Smile* on the other end. It doesn't come.

"Have you talked to yo beau yet?" my cousin Jennifer asks me. I can't remember if I called her or if she called me.
"No."
"Why not?" I can hear the judgment in her voice.
"I don't know," I begin to feel defensive. "I know he's probably out celebrating or something, you know."
"And he can't call you for a minute and say hi?"
I don't say anything.
"That's not fair to you."

My conversation with my cousin doesn't help. This is not how I imagined his first day out would be. I imagined that he would call me and we would spend all night talking on the phone, without any interruptions from that automated woman. Instead I am lying in my bed alone, wondering what's got *Mr. Beautiful Smile* so busy that he can't call me.

I call my friend Mike.

"Hey Mike, have you heard from *Mr. Beautiful Smile*?"

"Yeah, I talked to that nigga earlier today."

Everyone else heard from him, but me.

"Oh, I haven't heard from him at all today."

"Man you can't be like that. He just got out today. He probably out having some fun. Let that man be."

"What if that was you though?" I ask, trying to make him see where I'm coming from. "You wouldn't at least call me when you got out?"

"That nigga out having fun. That's what I would be doing. He's been locked up for three years."

"But you don't think that that's kind of messed up that he hasn't called me?"

"I mean yeah it is, but Jana` he's been in prison for three years…he'll call you eventually"

I hang up with Mike not feeling better at all. Something like a female's intuition kicks in. As I lie here in bed all alone, *Mr. Beautiful Smile* is out probably having sex with another girl. I can picture him kissing and touching some unknown, faceless woman.

I cry myself to sleep.

January 8, 2011:

"He's going to end up regretting it," I say still trying to comfort myself. "He's going to end up regretting that he didn't appreciate a girl like you." Someone who is loyal, always there for you, supportive, caring and loving. The pain still stays. And I pray to God that He would just make the pain go away. To please put me out of my misery. I start to hate love. I start wishing that I never fell in love in the first place because the heartache just doesn't seem to be worth it.

"I promise Jana`," I mange to say between sobs. "I promise that I will never put you through anything like this again." I will never put myself in another situation like this. I will never give someone my all. My love. My time. My dedication. My loyalty. And only to be unappreciated. Never again.

"It's ok Jana`," I say rocking myself. "Everything's going to be ok."

September 11, 2010:

My roommate and I are heading to Rivertown Mall to do a little shopping. I try to smile and maintain a conversation with her, but the fact that *Mr. Beautiful Smile* still hasn't called me makes it difficult to keep this charade up.

My cell phone rings. I look down to see a 313 number on the caller ID.

"Wasup Jana`," *Mr. Beautiful Smile*'s voice says.

"Hey." I want to ask why he hasn't called sooner, but it's not my place.

"My fault about not calling you last night," he says. "My phone was dead."

"Oh ok."

"But this my number so save it in yo phone."

"Ok."

"What you doing?"

"On my way to the mall with my roommate."

"Oh yeah," I hear a smile in his voice. "Make sure you buy me something."

"Yeah ok."

"But I'll call you later."

"Ok."

He never does.

September 15, 2010:

I wait at the Greyhound bus station in downtown Grand Rapids, standing in the late night heat. I am full of nerves. *Mr. Beautiful Smile* is spending three days with me at school. I finally get time with him, us all by ourselves. Something that I've waited for, for three years. As I spot the bus pulling up my heart begins to race double time. This moment is finally here. I go inside the bus station and spot him waiting with his suitcase for me. I walk up to him smiling. I wrap my arms around his neck, his around my waist. Our lips touch, this time without any correctional officers watching.

We walk over to Grand Valley's Grand Rapids campus talking about his time out so far.

"Give me a kiss," he says after we board the Westbound 50 Connector. I lean over and kiss him. This kiss is different. The kiss let me know what to expect once we were alone, in my apartment. We go through the bus ride holding hands and the butterflies in my stomach won't calm done for nothing.

Once we arrive to my apartment on the Allendale campus, I get *Mr. Beautiful Smile* something to eat and I go to the bathroom and change into my pjs. I think about him sitting there in my room, on my bed and the stomach butterflies go crazy. Twenty-two years old and I never had a guy alone in my room before.

I head into my room and see *Mr. Beautiful Smile* is dressed for bed, a white t-shirt and some basketball shorts. I cut off the light and climb in the bed with him.

"Goodnight," I say.

"Give me a goodnight kiss." We kiss. And then *Mr. Beautiful Smile's* firm hands explore my body. Heat rises from my body. My heart is pounding against my chest.

I give *Mr. Beautiful Smile* my virginity.

"We finally did it," he says after awhile.

I smile, my head resting on his chest. "Seems like it took forever, didn't it?"

He laughs a little. "Yeah, it did."

I sigh and smile as I feel his arm tighten around me. This is how I always imagined it, me lying in bed with the man that I love. I feel like I'm in a dream.

―――

January 8, 2011:

As I lay on my cousin's couch: my stomach jerking, my chest heaving, and I'm trying to catch my breath as tears stream down my face, I think about how things started going downhill after that moment.

I think about how the *very* next day *Mr. Beautiful Smile* tells me that he had sex with another girl on his first day out:

"Man, so many girls been acting like they want to [censored] with me," he says smiling, sitting next to me on my bed.

He's been saying this for awhile now and it makes me wonder. "Have you messed with any of them?" A part of me already knows the answer.

"Honestly?" he asks, as if he's now realizing his mistake.

I nod.

"Yeah."

I nod again, letting everything digest. "On yo first night out?" Again, a part of me already knows the answer.

He looks down at his phone. "Yeah."

A female's intuition is a mother. I wrap my arms around me. I feel used. Tricked. He said that he wouldn't have sex with me if he started messing around with other girls. He lied. It takes me a minute to bounce back from that let down.

"I won't regret my decision."

I think about the times he's made promises that he didn't keep:

"Of course I'mma call you," he says just a few days before he gets out of prison. "Why wouldn't I?"

"I just want to get my shit together first," he says the night I lost my virginity. "I want to get a car, a place to stay, some money, you know?" he looks down at me. "We're going to be together eventually."

"I swear man," he says recounting the $1,000 I loaned to him, leaving me with about $250 and about three-months of school left. "All you got to do is call me when you need some money and I got you."

"Whenever you need me I got you, cause you always been there for me."

"Yeah we gonna spend more time together," he says, answering my question about how it's going to be when I come home from school. "We going to be right around the corner from each other. Why wouldn't we?"

"I won't regret my decision."

I think about the times he's made me cry and let me down:

Just days after I gave him my virginity and all my money, he doesn't answer my calls or my texts.

The times that he's said that I'm getting on his nerves or irritating him.

The times I have to beg him to send me money for food.

The times I had to swallow my pride and ask family and friends for money for food and other expenses.

The times he wouldn't spend time with me.

The times he's said he just wasn't ready to be in a relationship.

The times he's said he just wasn't ready to be in a relationship.

And the low blow: the time I logged onto Facebook and read this:

"Why does it seem like I attract other niggaz women. Will I ever find the one for me??? I guess I'm looking for my miss anonymous. Simply Mr. Beautiful Smile."

"Will I ever find the one for me???" So, am I not the right one for him? My heart hurts. And something inside of me aches.

My stomach jerks, my chest heaves, and I try to catch my breath as tears stream down my face. My heart is broken.

"I won't regret my decision."

———

The things they advise me:

"Just fall back from him for a minute," my best friend says. "He'll realize how special you are eventually."
"You deserve better than him," a cousin says.
"There's basically two *Mr. Beautiful Smiles*, the prison one and the free one," my cousin's girlfriend says. "You basically fell in love with the prisoner *Mr. Beautiful Smile*."
"He just got out of prison man," a male cousin says.
"You just got to let him go," the same male cousin says. "And if y'all meant to be together he'll come back."
"You can't force me to be in a relationship with you," *Mr. Beautiful Smile* says. "It's just not going to work."
"At the end of the day," a friend says. "He was just another nigga."
"Start talking to other people."
"You should walk away."
"Leave him alone."
"Fall back!" the guarded side of me screams.

―――

Things I say to him:

"Hey," I text. "Can I come and see you today?"
"What are you doing?" I text.
I call.
I call.
I call.

"I feel like ever since you came home I've been slowly fading into the background and it seems like you just forgot all about me."

"I know we're not together, but I thought you would at least give me a little of your time and it hurts to see that you haven't."

"I would just like to spend some time with you."

"I understand you don't want to be in a relationship, I just thought you would've given me some time and it just seems like you don't want to talk to me anymore. Is that it?"

"I think I should just fall back and leave you alone."

"Hey, I won't bother you anymore," I text. "I just wanted to tell you to take care and stay out of trouble. I love you and always will, but I have to do what's best and fair for me. Goodbye."

———

Things he says to me:

"I'm not at home. I'll hit you up later." He never does.

He doesn't text back.

Voicemail.

Voicemail.

Voicemail.

"I've been a little busy, you right though. I apologize if I hurt your feelings, but I know I'm not ready to be in a relationship."

"I'm just not ready to be in a relationship."

"I'm just not ready to be in a relationship."

No response.

"I mean, do what you feel is best for you," he says nonchalantly.

He doesn't respond back.

January 8, 2011:

    I gather myself together. I sit up on my cousin's brown, suede couch—the feel of its soft cushion underneath my finger tips. My stomach stops jerking, my chest stops heaving, and I catch my breath as I wipe the tears that are streaming down my face. My heart *is* broken. Nothing is the way I thought it would be.
    I take a deep breath. "I won't regret my decision."

Death, Death and More Death

"Hello, my name is Jana`Chantel and I am addicted to death."

"Hello Jana`!" Although I can't see them, I can still feel their presence. I guess I'm at something like Deaths Anonymous.

"I-I just can't help it. I really don't mean to. I just end up thinking about it."

"Are you thinking about it now?" an authoritative voice asks me. And although the voice has some demand to it, there is still some sweetness and kindness behind it. So I can only assume that the voice is God and the others *must* be angels, former human beings whose minds had once been occupied with death.

"Yes," I confess. Of course I have to be cliché and envision myself lying down on a black leather couch, pouring my heart and soul to my therapist, who is God.

"And how do you see yourself dying now?"

"I'm being stabbed to death." I can feel the piercing stabs of a knife as it penetrates through my body. My stomach. My back. My neck. My chest. I heave and I try to catch my breath as I pull myself out of that vision. God just waits patiently as I gather myself together.

"What do you see?" he asks.

"I see a silhouette of a person. Maybe it's a man. Maybe it's a woman. The person breaks into my home and greets me in the kitchen as I am doing the dishes. They grab me by the neck. Two stabs to the stomach. One stab to the chest. A slit of the throat. I can feel the blood oozing out of me as my body drops to the floor." I again begin to calm myself down.

"*I see.*"

There is silence between us for awhile. God is allowing me to collect my thoughts.

"I feel like I'm going crazy."

"*Maybe you are.*"

"Maybe I am."

"*Maybe you aren't,*" God contradicts.

Silence.

"I just can't help it. If someone else was in my situation, I'm *sure* they would be thinking about death too."

"*And by your 'situation' you mean your mother being killed?*"

"Yes."

"*And your father dying from cancer?*"

"Yes."

"*And you getting shot?*"

"Yes."

"*I see.*"

"Do you?"

God laughs. "*My child, I created you. I am the one who put you in this 'situation',*" he laughs again. "*Of course I see, more clearly than you can.*"

I sigh. "You're right."

Silence.

"I feel like I am going crazy."

"*I don't think you're crazy.*"

"Thank-you."

"You're just not normal," God assures me.

"How could I be?" I say a little offended. "Nothing I've been through *was* normal."

"You're right."

"And besides, no one is normal."

"You're right about that too."

"And what *is* normal anyways?"

"That is a good question."

I sigh. "Hello, my name is Jana` Chantel and I am addicted to death."

"Hello Jana`!"

"I-I just can't help it. I really don't mean to. I just end up thinking about it," I say again in an all white room. The only thing of color is a black leather couch that I lay on. And although I am alone, I can feel the presence of God and other angels around me. I have to wonder if I am straddling the line between life and death. Heaven and Hell. And I have to be cliché yet again and say that the room that I lay in is something like a purgatory, or maybe it *is* purgatory.

"Are you thinking about it now?"

"Yes."

"And how do you see yourself dying now?"

"I get struck by a stray bullet." I try really hard not to panic as I feel that familiar burning, vibrational feeling enter my body.

"What do you see?"

"I'm walking on a street in Detroit. My headphones are blaring, playing some random song that comes on the radio. I never hear the gunshot. I just feel a burning, vibrating feeling go through the left side of my chest. Like a tree that's been chopped, my body hits the concrete."

"I see." A part of me feels that he *actually* does see.

"Why do I feel so crazy?"

"Why don't you tell me?"

"Do you think about death?" I ask God.

"Yes."

"All the time?"

God laughs, a musical tone. *"My child, I have to see that my children make it home."*

"Every day?"

"Yes."

"Of every second?"

"Yes."

"Then I guess you can understand me," I say a little disappointed. I was sure that *no one*, not even God, could *really* understand what I am going through.

"I guess I can."

"But have you intended to do that though?" I ask out of curiosity. "Create humans who are so obsessed with death?"

"I created you didn't I?"

I shrug. "Just seems like there was some type of error there."

"My child, I don't make mistakes."

I sigh. "I just don't want to feel like I'm going crazy anymore."

"And you feel like you're crazy because you think about death so often?"

"Yes."

Silence.

"Am I crazy?"

"I don't think you are."

"I'm just not normal?"

"You're not normal," God confirms.

"But what is normal?"
"Maybe the feeling of insanity."
"Maybe."
Silence.

"Hello, my name is Jana` Chantel and I am addicted to death," I say for the third time.

"Hello Jana`!"

"I-I just can't help it. I really don't mean to. I just end up thinking about it."

"Are you thinking about it now?"

"Yes."

"And how do you see yourself dying now?"

"A car accident."

"What do you see?"

"I am on the freeway, I-275 heading south to be more exact. My auntie and I are heading to the mall out in Novi. It's a sunny day. There's a semi-truck in front of us that is carrying some steel poles on its flatbed. The truck hits a pot hole and the chains that are holding the poles together break. The poles scatter all over the road and cars swerve all over the freeway. One of the poles bounces off the truck and comes towards our car. My auntie tries to swerve out of the way, but not quick enough. A pole comes through the passenger side window and rips through my chest. It pins me to my seat. My auntie's screams are the last thing I hear."

"I see."

I laugh, which seems a little inappropriate at this moment. I can feel God and his angels giving me a questioning look. "It seems like a scene out of that movie *Final Destination*," I explain. "You know, where a group of people 'cheat' death and death ends up haunting them."

God remains silent, allowing me time to recollect myself.

"You think that's what's happening to me?"

"Death haunting you?"

"Yeah."

God is silent for a moment. *"You think you cheated death?"*

"Yes."

"And you're talking about when you got shot?"

"Yes."

God remains silent.

"Is there such a thing as cheating death?"

God laughs that musical laugh of his. *"My child, as I've said before, I don't make mistakes."*

"So, you intended for me to survive then?"

"I did."

"Why?"

"Don't go dwelling on reasons," he warns me. *"Many people have gone crazy doing that."*

"But aren't I already crazy?"

God laughs again.

"So you must have a purpose for me then?"

"I do."

"Which is?"

"My child, you will know what it is when I get you there."

"So I'm not there yet?" I ask. "At my destination?"

"You will know when you get there."

I sigh. God can be complicated at times. "Hello, my name is Jana` Chantel and I am addicted to death," I say yet again.

"Hello Jana`!" Sometimes I forget that they're there. God has a way of making you feel comfortable when you're pouring your heart out to him. Although he already knows what's going on through your mind.

"I-I just can't help it. I really don't mean to. I just end up thinking about it."

"Are you thinking about it now?"

"Yes."

"And how do you see yourself dying now?"

"I have an asthma attack."

"Ah, something I gave you." I can hear a smile in his voice. *"What do you see?"*

"I'm sleeping, but the difficulty of breathing wakes me. It feels like an elephant is sitting on my chest and I reach for my inhaler. I give myself four puffs and wait for the medicine to kick in, but it doesn't happen. I try another four puffs of my inhaler and still nothing. The difficulty of breathing intensifies. I try to dial for help, but my body goes weak. I know that I am not getting enough oxygen. I keep trying to catch my next breath, but it never comes."

"I see."

"I know you do," I confess.

Silence.

"So am I having a psychotic break or something?"

"Why do you ask that?"

"Well," I say realizing the nature of this conversation. "This isn't real, right?"

"Why isn't it?"

"Well, this is all in my head, right?" God has a way of making you feel like you're sane when you feel like you aren't.

"And that doesn't make it real?"

"I'm not really sure. I don't think it is."

"It's real if you think it is."

"So this is real?" I say sounding redundant.

"I don't see why it can't be."

"Well, this can't be normal."

"Nothing is normal," God says a-matter-of-factly.

"But are you really here?"
"I am everywhere my child."
"And you're here to help me?"
"Do you feel like you need help?"
"Yes."
"There's nothing wrong with thinking about death."
"It is if you think about it so often."
"Are you afraid of death?" I've been waiting for God to ask me this question, even though I know he already knows the answer. *"Afraid of dying?"*
"No."
"So, what is the problem?"
"My addiction!" I feel like he's not getting it. I wish to be cured. "I am consumed by it! So consumed that I do it subconsciously!"
God is silent.
"Please," I begin to feel like I'm going to cry. "Please, I don't want to be crazy anymore."
"My child, death is a part of life. Why are you crazy because you think about it so much?"
"Because this isn't normal."
"But you aren't normal."
"I just don't want to be crazy anymore."
Silence.
"I just don't want to be crazy anymore."
Silence.
"I just don't want to be crazy anymore."
God remains silent. I am right on the edge of breaking down and crying when I realize something. "My child, I don't make mistakes," rings through my head and I realize that God has intended for me to be this way. I wipe away the few tears that escaped from my eyes.
I take a deep breath. "Hello, my name is Jana` Chantel and I am addicted to death."

"Hello Jana`," God says calmly.
"I-I just can't help it. I really don't mean to. I just end up thinking about it."

Things My Father Taught Me

"Right...left...right...left...jab...upper cut...hook!" my dad's voice rings in my ears as my seven-year-old self hits the big black punching bag in our basement. My little fists are clenched tightly in blue boxing gloves as I execute the moves my dad commands. The smell of moth balls and aged wood saturate my nose as I throw a right...left...right...left...jab...upper cut...hook. Sunlight peaks through the basement windows bringing warmth to its cold, darkness. The weights, work out station and the entertainment system become brighter as the yellow light hits them.

"Right...left...right...left...jab...upper cut...hook!" I feel his presence to the left of me, watching me execute the moves, making sure that as time moves on I will always know how to protect myself.

"Right...left...right...left...jab...upper cut...hook!" My little fists keep punching the bag the way he tells me. My breathing is getting faster, arms, weaker, but I keep punching away.

"Stop," my dad says. "Come here."

I walk over to him, my chest heaving up and down. He looks at me intently, his dark brown eyes looking me over.

"Guards up," he commands.

I pull my fists just inches away from my face, creating a box-like figure. My dad leans down towards me and locks his hands around my wrists. He pulls me closer to him.

"Never start a fight," he advices me. "But *always* protect yourself."

    I stand in our bathroom's doorway watching my dad cut my cousin's hair. I watch as he bites his tongue and takes the clippers through my cousin's head. I smile. My dad stands out in the pink/peach colored bathroom. The bright color of the bathroom contrasts against his dark, chocolate skin.

    He looks up at me and sees me watching him. He gives me that smile that I love so much, a flash of his straight, pearly white teeth. I hear my other cousins throughout the house, laughing and playing. It is a common thing for him to get all of my cousins and have them spend the weekend at our house. They're not as fortunate as me and my brother. Their fathers aren't present in their lives. So my dad steps up and becomes that male figure.

    My dad finishes cutting my cousin's hair and brushes the falling pieces of hair off of his neck. My cousin hurries up and jumps out of the chair.

    "Get back here boy," my dad says in that authoritative voice of his. I smile a little because I know what's coming next; it's a ritual of his.

    My cousin groans, "Aww, Uncle James," he slowly climbs back in the chair.

    My dad gives his devious smile and pretends like he's spitting into his hand. My cousin scrunches up his face in anticipation. My dad stretches his hand back and smacks the back of my cousin's freshly cut head. My cousin flinches up, frowns, and then rubs the back of his head as he climbs out the chair. My dad looks over at me and smiles.

"Who's next?"

I sit in the living room on my dad's lap. He wears a white beater and blue jean shorts. He makes his muscles in his chest jump and I try to hit them, always missing the side that jumped. I laugh as I play the game that we always play. My dad smiles at me and runs his fingers through my hair.

"My little princess," he says. I smile and rest my head on his chest. He takes my chin and makes me look at him. "A man should always treat you like the queen you are."

**

I stand in the kitchen later on that day and watch as my dad and stepmom argue. Over what, I'm not sure. But I realize then that there are two sides to a person: a good side and a bad side. Right now I am witnessing the bad side of my dad. I watch silently as my dad pushes my stepmom up against the wall and slaps her repeatedly. I flinch every time he delivers the blows. For a moment his eyes meet mine, and what he said earlier enters my mind, *"A man should always treat you like the queen you are."* I realize right there, at the age of seven, that a man should *never* put his hands on his queen.

We're leaving my grandmother's house. I sit in the back of the 1980 silver, burgundy soft-top Lincoln.

The blue cushions from the seat softly rub up against my leg. We head down Wilfred towards Gratiot. My dad stops and waits to turn left onto Gratiot. I look out the window, looking out at the residents of Detroit. Some people sit on their porch staring out into the nothingness. Some people just walk up and down the street, as if they're wasting their life away.

I see girls walking the streets, their bodies barely covered with cloths. Guys look at them with lust in their eyes. My dad looks at me through the rear view mirror. I meet his eyes.

"Your body is a temple," he says as he drives off casually. "You should always treat it as such." I nod at him and try to get a last look at the girls. At seven-years-old I let the view sink in and I let my dad's advice sink in. I vow to always treat my body like the temple it is.

"Ouch....ouch!" I cry as my dad runs the comb through my head. I am eight-years-old and my stepmom and my dad have been separated for a while now. "Ouch...ouch...OUCH!"

"I'm sorry baby," my dad says as he pats my back to comfort me. He picks up the comb and runs it gently through my head. But my tender headedness makes his effort seem in vain.

"Ouch!"

"I know, I'm sorry baby," he continues to say as he styles my hair.

**

The next day at school everyone comments on how pretty my hair is, something that really hasn't been done before. As my brother and I start walking home from school, a classmate's father stops me.

"Your hair is very pretty," he says, his daughter right in toe. "Who did it?"

"My daddy."

He looks surprised for a moment; as if he couldn't believe that a man did *that* job.

"Your daddy did that?" he asks in disbelief.

I nod.

"Well, he did an excellent job," he says amazed.

As my brother and I begin to walk home I think, *"A good father does hair well."*

We're invited to go to church with my dad's cousin. The church is called Greater Grace Temple and it is the biggest church I've ever seen. The atmosphere is welcoming and comforting. The way that the choir sings and the preacher preaches just moves people, moves people so much that my dad ends up getting baptized.

After that Sunday, after his baptism, I see a change in my dad. He's calmer. Peaceful. He's different. And I learn that people can eventually change for the better.

It's the worst sight that an eight-year-old, daddy's little girl could see. As my brother and I walk home from school I spot a police car sitting in front of our house. My heart races. My brother and I begin to pick up the pace. As I get closer to the house I see my dad sitting in the back seat handcuffed and next door neighbors have gathered to witness the scene.

"Daddy," I say my voice panicked and my heart racing. "Daddy."

"It's ok," he says trying to reassure us, but the way he's looking down and avoiding looking at us says otherwise. I can tell that he's ashamed that his children have to see him in this position, witness him being the victim of the system.

"Daddy," tears stream from my eyes.

"Look," he says in a voice that tells me to pull myself together. "Y'all go with her," he nods to a woman who's standing not too far from us. I glance over at her for the first time. She's about 5'1, chubby, brown skin with short gray hair. She wears a smile on her face, but it is a strained one, as if she knows the tension of the situation.

"Go with her," my dad says in his commanding voice. "Go with her until y'all auntie comes."

I nod silently, trying to hold back my tears. My brother and I step back towards our neighbor. The officer pushes my dad into the car and gets ready to close the door.

"Everything's fine," he says again. "Everything's ok."

We all sit at my great-aunt's house. My brother and I sit on her couch watching TV while my dad and my great-aunt talk for a moment in the kitchen. It's been a few weeks since the incident with my dad and the police. My brother and I still don't know what all happened, just that my stepmom called the police on my dad.

"James and Jana`," my dad calls as he and my great-aunt come out of the kitchen and into the living room. My brother and I give our dad our undivided attention. Our great-aunt sits down on a chair and cuts off the TV.

My dad looks back and forth between my brother and me. "If anything ever happens to me, I want y'all to live with y'all auntie Daune." Hearing this scares me. It's like a warning sign that he's not going to be here much longer.

My brother and I remain silent.

"Do y'all understand me?" he says in his stern voice. "When I'm gone, y'all are to go with y'all auntie Daune and no one else."

"We understand daddy," I say. I'm trying hard not to cry. I know that he's not going to be around much longer.

I'm about to get a whipping. I'm not clear as to what I did, just that something didn't get done and now I'm about to pay for it. I don't get in trouble that often, but when I do it's terrifying.

"Get in here," my dad says in his angry voice. Tears automatically start to fall. Not for sympathy, but because of genuine fear.

"I'm sorry," I say, pleading as I slowly walk into my dad's room.

"Turn around," I hear him slam his bedroom door.

I start to cry harder and my heart starts to race as I turn around towards the bed.

"Hands on the bed."

I hold my breath as I feel him swing the belt back. I feel the whack of his black leather belt make contact with my behind. I cry even harder as I feel whack, after whack, after whack. The stinging of the belt becomes unbearable and I run away from the next whack. My dad runs after me and catches me. The way he throws me on the floor and pins me down tells me that this upset him even more.

"You little BITCH!!!" he yells as he continues to hit me with the belt. Although I am still kicking and screaming, a part of me goes numb inside because all I can hear in my head is *"You little BITCH!!!"* and the anger that's behind it. And it seems like I'm kicking and screaming because of the pain that this is causing me.

After my whipping I go to my room and cry as I lay in my bed. I'm in disbelief. In all of my eight-years I have never heard my dad speak to me in that way. He always had such high respect for me and always treated me like a princess. The stinging of my behind doesn't hurt as bad as my heart.

**

Later on in the day my dad calls me back into his room. I sit on the edge of his bed with my head hanging low. I feel him looking at me, but I keep my eyes on the floor.

"I'm sorry," he says lifting up my chin. "For calling you out yo name."

I remain silent, but I see pain behind his eyes.

"A man should *never* disrespect you like that," he says sternly, as if he's teaching his self this lesson too.

I nod slowly.

"Will you forgive me?" I hear fear in his voice.

"Yes daddy."

He hugs me and I wrap my arms tightly around him. I wipe the last of my tears, never forgetting the day that my daddy hurt me.

He holds up a small clear plastic bag that contains the remains of my mother's jewelry. I sit on his bed watching as he holds it up, giving me that stern look of his.

"When I'm gone, you are to get this jewelry," he says. "You and *only* you."

"Ok."

"I'm going to hide it. And when I'm gone you come and get it." He hides the bag in the folds of the curtain at the top of his bedroom window. "Don't tell anyone. You just go and get your jewelry. You got it?"

"Yes," I hate when he talks like this. I don't want to think about him no longer being around, but I know the things that he's telling me are important. And sadly, his time on this earth is drawing to an end.

"Good, come here," he gives me a hug and kisses me on the forehead.

**

A few weeks later I sit on the same bed in the exact same spot as if nothing's changed. But so much has changed. The man who has taught me everything is no longer here. Gone. Never coming back. He finally lost his battle with cancer. And now I sit on the bed numb. Empty. It feels like my heart and half of my soul have been taken away from me. My title of a daddy's little girl has been ripped away from me.

To make matters worse, I hear my grandmother and her sisters downstairs tearing the house up looking for things. I know what they're looking for.

"Don't tell anyone. You just go and get your jewelry," my dad's instructions ring through my ears.

I remain sitting on the bed listening to my father's mother and his aunts tear up his home, taking the remaining of his worldly possessions. Surprisingly, I'm not shocked. I just sit there silently listening, patiently waiting.

After they take all that they can, they leave. My auntie and uncle look both angry and disgusted.

"I can't believe them," my auntie says. I can tell by her face that she is irritated and fed-up.

"You know what they was looking for?" my uncle says.

"Yeah I know, Gwen's jewelry," my auntie's pissed that they were trying to take what was rightfully mine.

"He hid it," I say, it seems like for the first time since we got there.

"You know where?" my auntie asks.

I nod. "He showed me."

"Where?" my uncle asks.

I hesitate. "He told me not to tell anyone." Even when he's gone, I'm afraid to disobey him.

My uncle laughs. "Man ain't nobody gonna try and take it from you."

I sigh and point to the top of the curtains on the bedroom window. "It's in the folds." My uncle reaches up and takes my mother's jewelry down. He hands it to me. I tightly grasp it in my hands.

As I clench onto my mother's last worldly possessions, my father's last warning rings through my head.

"Don't tell anyone. You just go and get your jewelry."

At eight-years-old I realize that my father was preparing me for the cruelness of this world.

Years have passed since my father died, about ten years to be exact. I'm eighteen and I'm in my freshmen year in college at Clark Atlanta University. But for some reason I find myself back in Michigan. Although I'm in a store, a grocery store to be more specific, something tells me that I'm back in Detroit. And then my heart skips a few beats as I see a dark chocolate man walking around the produce section with a small basket on his arm. He looks up at me and smiles that beautiful smile of his.

I start to run towards him. "Daddy!!!!" I yell. My voice sounds like I'm eight-years-old again.

He laughs and hugs me. "Hey baby," he looks me over "Wow, you are so beautiful."

I give him a shy smile. He has a way of making me feel like a little princess again. We walk around the produce section for a little bit. He occasionally looks over at me and smiles and then continues to pick out his fruit. By the layout of the store I realize that we're at the Farmer Jacks on West Outer Drive near the Southfield freeway. This assures me that this is a dream because Farmer Jacks has been out of business for awhile now. But I don't care. I'm glad to see him, a feeling I haven't felt since he left.

"My baby is in college!" he yells out suddenly. I laugh. "Man I'm so proud of you!" He gives me a hug and a kiss on my forehead.

"Thanks daddy."

He shakes his head. "My baby is in *college.* That is amazing. You out here doing ya thang."

"Yeah," I say smiling.

"Me and yo mama are so proud of you." We walk down the aisle with the cookies and crackers. He picks up some Chips Ahoy and puts them in his basket.

He notices my silence. "How you doing?" As if he doesn't know already.

"I'm good."

He looks at me for a moment and smiles. "I raised a strong woman."

I smile.

"You like Atlanta?"

"So far."

"Just make sure them niggas down there treat you like the queen you are."

I laugh. "I won't have it any other way."

He laughs. We continue to shop and talk. At the end, I pay for his groceries.

We sit in the stanking Lincoln (as my auntie calls it) in front of my on-campus apartments at Grand Valley State University. I sit behind the driver's seat and my dad sits in the passenger's. The blue cushions of the seat are soft like I remember.

"So you like this guy huh?" my daddy asks about *Mr. Beautiful Smile*. He's acting nonchalant, but I can tell that he has some kind of feeling towards it.

"I love him," I admit. I watch as his beautiful face strains a little. I smile. The lump that used to be on the left side of his neck is no longer there. I'm glad to see it gone. It lets me know that he's no longer in pain.

"You love him huh?" he asks playing with his hands. Even in *this* situation, it's hard for him to see his 21-year-old daughter in love with another man.

I laugh. "He's not a bad guy daddy."

"Nah, he seems to be a good guy. I'm not in the position to judge him." My dad use to sell drugs too, so I guess he couldn't say too much about *Mr. Beautiful Smile* being in prison for it.

"Daddy," I say, trying to pull him out of the funk he's in. "You're still my number one man."

He smiles at me and then he laughs as if I told him a joke. "I don't have anything to worry about."

"Why you say that?"

"Because Doug is going to give him hell."

I sigh as I realize that he's right. My granddad took my dad's place and now all my male suitors have to go through him, which is no easy task. "You're right," I groan a little.

My daddy continues to laugh and doubles over. I give him the evil eye.

He tries to straighten up a little. He holds my chin. "Aww, my poor baby."

"Not funny daddy."

I watch him laugh for the rest of my dream.

Lately, my dad hasn't visited me, but it doesn't mean that there are things that I don't need to learn. There were times that I've longed for him, cried for him, and wished that he was here to help me out and give me advice, I think about the lessons that he taught while he was here. Life is a constant fight, a lesson that he's taught me well. So sometimes you have to come with a right…left…right…left…jab…upper cut…hook.

Like Mother, Like Daughter

A Case Study of Love

Subjects Profile:

Gwen Felicia
- Mother
- Age: 19-20
- In love with: James Cardell, drug dealer

Jana Chantel
- Daughter
- Age: 21-22
- In love with: *Mr. Beautiful Smile*, prisoner (convicted of selling drugs) and ex-convict

Case Study Background:

      Although their time with each other was limited, there seems to be a lot of similarities between mother, Gwen Felicia, and her daughter, Jana` Chantel. One of these tragedies is getting shot, which, sadly led to Gwen Felicia's death. Looking at documents written by both women, it appears they had similarities with love as well.

      Gwen was in love with a drug dealer and, ironically, Jana` Chantel fell for a guy who sold drugs too. But, did Jana`'s relationship end like her mother's?

Gwen Felicia[2]:

April Tue. 26, 88

    James is mad at me. He seems to think I don't love him anymore. I love this man more than life itself. The way I feel for him I never dreamed I could love this way.

    I know I haven't been with a lot of guys and some people will even go as far and say how do I know my love for him is true. When the chips were down I was always by his side. Bad or good we were together.

    I wonder how he could doubt my love for him. I'll walk through fire for him. I sometimes doubt his love, but deep down inside I know his love is true.

Jana` Chantel[3]:

Feb. 4, 2010   Thu. 9:37 p.m.

    What can I say, besides the fact that I love [*Mr. Beautiful Smile*]. I never felt this way about any guy before. He's a great person. He's always so sweet to me and he treats me with a lot of respect.

    I went to go see him [in prison] on Sunday 1/24/10 and on 1/31/10. The first time I went to go see

---

    [2] Note: Dairy entries appear the same as they were written.

    [3] Note: Jana` Chantel's diary entries are not in chronological order.

him I was so nervous because I hadn't seen him in 2 ½ years. I was so comfortable around him though, which was a good.

I feel really good about our relationship. We both hope that we'll be together for awhile.

Gwen Felicia:

Fri. May 6, 1988
       Time: 12:26 a.m.

I love James so much and I love it when he acts so nice to me.

Jana` Chantel:

Feb. 4, 2010   Thu. 9:37 p.m.

I think about my mom and dad and can't help but wonder if this was the kind of love they had for one another. It probably was, even stronger than *Mr. Beautiful Smile* and I love for each other. I want their kind of love (just not the way it ended).

Gwen Felicia:

May 9 Mon. 88
       Time: 11:33 p.m.

James and I got into a little argument. James was very upset because [my sister] said "Little James don't hardly look like you." He accused me of [censored] June and he said June told me about [James' baby mama] when James was the only one who told me.

We were on the freeway and James discovered that [his baby mama] and her friends was following us. They drove up on the side of us and I looked right into the car. [James' baby mama] and her friends drove in front of us and then James discovered their car. He speeded up to catch them and they speeded up and got away.

This really made me upset, I mean what's going on? This really makes me wonder. Something else that burns me up is I don't have anyone to talk to that won't tell what I say. I have to keep everything to myself, bottled up inside. It drives me crazy. I just wish I find me a true blue friend.

Jana` Chantel:

March 7, 2010　　　　　　　　　　　Sun. 9:22 p.m.

So I might as well tell you what's been going on with [*Mr. Beautiful Smile*] and I since the last time. Well, I haven't seen him since [Feb. 14, 2010] sadly. And we got into an argument. I didn't like that.

He was having a bad day and took it out on me. He was talking about doing something that I didn't want him to do. I was trying to change the subject (so we wouldn't argue) by asking him how he would feel about me going to London for an internship, but it back fired on me.

He got really mad and thought that I brought that up to upset him. I did it to avoid an argument, but that didn't happen.

Gwen Felicia:

May 15 Sun. 88
　　　　Time: 12:44 a.m.

Well everything has been going well.

We took [our godson] home today, came back and [censored], it was good as hell.

Jana` Chantel:

Sep. 28, 2010　　　　　　　　Tue. 10:24 p.m.

I end up losing my virginity to [*Mr. Beautiful Smile*] (Sep. 15, 2010). I liked it. I thought it was pretty good (even though I was probably bad at it).

Gwen Felicia:

Sun. July 3, 88
　　　　Time: 1:30 a.m.

Me and James had a fight, he bruised my face and body pretty bad. I know he loves me and don't really mean to hurt me. I don't know it seems we need a little time apart.

He be gone a lot and I miss him. I guess you can say I'm crazy about being under him. James really understands some of my ways. I'm a little hard to understand.

Jana` Chantel:

March 7, 2010   Sun. 9:22 p.m.

But we worked [our argument] out. [*Mr. Beautiful Smile*] said that I should apply for the internship in London. And he apologized for hurting my feelings.

I think he's getting better at reading me. Although I wouldn't admit it, he could tell that he hurt my feelings. He felt bad for it too. But it's fine. I still love him anyway. And we're fine now.

Gwen Felicia:

Mon. July 18, 1988
    Time: 8:55 p.m.

Lately James and I haven't been getting along very well because of [his friend] and this makes me hate him more each day.

James seems to think I'm actually messing around with him. I would never do anything like that to him. He will never ever trust me, but yet he loves me yeah right.

Jana` Chantel:

Sep. 28, 2010   Tue. 10:24 p.m.

So *Mr. Beautiful Smile* got out [from prison] on Sep. 10, 2010. I was glad about that. But I found out that he had sex with another girl that day (I wasn't *too* happy about that). I had hoped that I would at least be the first person he had sex with when he got out.

I don't know though. It seemed like after [we had sex], he's been distancing his self away from me. When I call him I always get his voicemail and when I text him he doesn't respond back. It hurts because I feel like he's avoiding me or something.

Gwen Felicia:

Tues. July 26, 88
    Time: 12:43 a.m.

James doesn't understand me. He sometimes talk to me like I'm a kid and this make me upset, but he see his view.

Today I was driving out the driveway and the way the cars were parked it would have been hard for me to get out. Instead of James saying nicely use the people driveway he has to fuss.

James makes me upset sometimes and when I show the way I feel we have to fight. I try to hold it inside and be depressed when we fight. I feel I can't win.

Jana` Chantel:

Sep. 28, 2010　　　　　　　　　Tue. 10:24 p.m.

[*Mr. Beautiful Smile*] told me yesterday that he was coming up here to see me today. I had texted him early this morning to see if he was still coming and he said later. Well, when it got closer to the time my class starts I called him to see if he was still coming and he told me a later time.

I told him that he could've called and told me that. Then he got all mad and was like I'm irritating him and getting on his nerves.

He's said that to me a few times now and it makes me feel really bad. It seems like everything I do and everything I say irritates him.

Gwen Felicia:

Fri. July 30, 88
　　　Time: 10:28 p.m.

Well me and James broke up again today but we are back together. James still accuses me of fooling around with [James' friend]. I hate [James' friend] more each day. He's the one who started this shit.

I love James with all my heart and I would never do anything like that with his best friend. I wouldn't like him to do that to me.

Mom says you should always try to be true to the one you love. Your heart should belong to one man only.

My heart belongs to James and James only. So far for 4 yrs. my heart and I has been true.

Jana` Chantel:

July 11, 2010   Sun. 5:42 p.m.

Mr. Beautiful Smile tells me that we shouldn't be together when he gets out [of prison]. He said that he knows that he will be having sex with other girls. I'm really hurt about that. I feel like I've been waiting for him all this time and I *still* have to wait to be with him.

Gwen Felicia:

Aug. 1 Mon. 1988
       Time: 10:56 p.m.

I went to the doc. today he said "the baby is in position." James and I think it's gonna come early. This is a problem. James is still having money problems and this adds to this problem. I often wish my shower was a success then he wouldn't have to worry.

I feel bad worrying James about money. I wish there was something I could do.

God I know material things should not be asked for, but God please bless James and help him out please God let him make the money for his bills please God. God please help him get back on his feet.

I know what James does to make his money is against your law Lord and I ask you to forgive him for that. Lord please let luck ride on his side for awhile.

Jana` Chantel:

Feb. 10, 2010   Wed. 8:23 p.m.

I'm worried about *Mr. Beautiful Smile*. He called me today saying that he was stressed out. He really doesn't want to get into trouble when he gets out. He doesn't want to be around the area where he can get into trouble.

I think he feels that if he is around me then he won't get into any trouble, that's why he doesn't like the fact that I'll still be in school when he gets out. I just pray that he'll be strong enough to wait a few months until I graduate.

Gwen Felicia:

Saturday October 8, 1988

  A lot has been going on. I had my baby Jana` Chantel on Aug. 17, 1988 Wed. 2:50 p.m. at Sinai. James didn't act so exciting. We have our fights again. He thinks I [censored] [his friend] "No way!"

  James act real funny now he tries to keep his phone calls a secret. He talks to [my best friend] a lot. I no longer trust him. He can steal my friends away. If I talk to [his friend] I got to be [censored] him in James eyes. I don't talk to him.

Jana` Chantel:

Oct. 1, 2010   Fri. 12:22 p.m.

  Yesterday (Sep. 30) *Mr. Beautiful Smile* came out to see me. He came with two friends. When we were at a store one of his friends asked what I do to *Mr. Beautiful Smile* because he's sprung. He said that *Mr. Beautiful Smile* always be talking about trying to come out here to see me.

  This kind of threw me for a loop because to me, *Mr. Beautiful Smile* doesn't act like he's sprung over me. I don't know. *Mr. Beautiful Smile* seemed embarrassed when his friend said that to me. I don't know. A part of me doesn't want to believe it because I don't want to end up getting hurt if I find out otherwise.

A part of me feels really bad for feeling this way and doubting his feelings that he may have for me. I mean, I don't doubt his love for me, I *know* he loves me. It's just the extent of his love I doubt. I just don't want to get hurt so I'm trying to protect myself so I can cushion the fall if it *should* ever come.

Gwen Felicia:

Sunday Oct. 9, 1988
      Time: 12:40 a.m.

James and I are getting along. He's trying to get things back together. James wants to be the perfect father for his children. God please let things go well for him this time.

Jana` Chantel:

Jan. 8, 2011   Sat. 3:27 p.m.

Today I came to the conclusion that I should leave *Mr. Beautiful Smile* alone and just fall back.

Gwen Felicia:

Sat. Oct. 15, 88

A Homemade Card Reads:

James,

I want to tell you in my own words how much I love you.

James you came into my life and changed me around. You made me a better person. You taught me how to love. You taught me how to care and share. James you showed me how to have a good time. You took me to places I've never seen or been. You taught me how to make love. James you brought me things that I dreamed of. You gave me a beautiful home. You gave me two beautiful sons. Most of all you gave me a beautiful daughter of my very own. Important of all you gave me your love and you.

Jana` Chantel:

July 6, 2011   Wed. 11: 14 p.m.

I write stories about [*Mr. Beautiful Smile*]: "Because They Said That Good Things Will Come to Those Who Wait," "Still Waiting For Good Things To Come," and "Like Mother, Like Daughter: A Case Study of Love" because I still love him and a small part of me still hopes that we will be together some day.[4]

---

[4] Sadly enough on Monday July 25, 2011 at approximately 10:10 a.m. subject Jana` Chantel finds out that *Mr. Beautiful Smile* is in a relationship (it isn't with her).

Case Study Conclusion:

While Gwen and James' relationship ended with Gwen's death, Jana` and *Mr. Beautiful Smile's* ended, or should I say never began, because she wasn't what he really wanted.

Things Left Unsaid

When I was thirteen, my brother accidentally shot me.

**

"I was standing in the living room...," I say to the police as I lay in my bed. With the help from my cousin Javon, I was able to get from the floor of the living room to my bed. A few minutes ago I was trying to go to sleep and wishing that it all was just a dream.

"Ma'am," one of the officers says which I find kind of ironic since I'm thirteen. "What happened?"

"I was standing in the living room...," I repeat, but again I stop right there. The lie my cousin Noland wanted me to tell the police couldn't pass my lips, only the truthful part could come out.

"There are no bullet holes coming into the house indicating a drive by," another officer says as he walks into my bedroom. A hole has just been punched into the lie that Noland wanted me to tell.

"Ma'am what happened?" the officer asks again.

"Please," for the first time tears fall. "I just want to go to the hospital." The bullet that ripped through my body several minutes ago is still a huge concern to me. "I'll tell you everything after I go to the hospital."

"No," the officer says casually, as if my life wasn't depending on it. "We need to know what happened first."

I lay in my bed crying torn with a difficult decision: dying or giving up my brother.

"I was standing in the living room…"

Surprisingly enough, the officer just sighs and allows the paramedics to put me on the stretcher and wheel me out to the ambulance. I shut my eyes tightly, not wanting to see my gawking neighbors.

"I was in my house," I hear a neighbor say. "When I heard just *one* gunshot."

The paramedics load me in the back of the ambulance and I begin to think that everything is going to be ok, until I realize that we are not moving.

"Jana` sweetie," I hear a female voice say, which is a little strange since I know that both of the paramedics are male. "I'm detective…" I kind of block out her name from there. "Sweetie we need to know what happened."

"Please," I cry again. "I just want to go to the hospital."

"I know sweetie, but we can't let you go until you tell us what happened."

Time is of the essence and it is slowly slipping away from me as I continue to stay here.

I give in. "My brother was playing with a gun and it went off…he didn't mean it."

As the sirens begin to sound and the ambulance speeds off all I could think is, "James I hope you forgive me."

**

When I was thirteen, my brother accidentally shot me.

**

However, according to the *Detroit Free Press* and various news-casters we fought over the gun. Apparently, there was some type of a struggle and I jumped on my brother's back trying to get the gun away from him when he shot me.

So far from the truth.

Actually, we were just standing in the living room. Standing in the living room and yes he had a gun in his hand; a thirteen year old feels like he has all the power in the world with a gun in his hands. I wasn't thinking. He was my brother and he had a gun.

He said something that was funny. Something that made me laugh and then...BOOM!

That was it. An honest *accident*.

**

When I was thirteen, my brother accidentally shot me.

**

This is the worst day of my life, which says a lot since I am currently spending the summer recovering from a gunshot injury. I sit on the witness stand fidgeting with my fingers.

"Ms. Chantel," the prosecutor says. "Is the person who shot you in this room?"

I don't want to be here. But I've been made to. My auntie told me that I could get into trouble if I didn't come to testify. Testify against my own brother. It seems like no one is listening to me. It was an accident. Just an accident. I'm not mad at him and I feel like no one else should be either.

The prosecutor gives me this waiting look. I sigh and reluctantly say "Yes."

"And can you point to him please."

I slowly lift up my arm and point to my brother. My arm feels a thousand times heavier.

"Let the record show that she is pointing to the defendant."

I frown.

"And Ms. Chantel were you _____ from this incident?"

I didn't catch what he said and couldn't understand his question. So out of protective instincts I say "No."

He gives me a patronizing look and then smiles. "Let me rephrase it, did you sustain any injuries from this incident?"

I frown and regrettably say "Yes."

"Thank you Ms. Chantel," he looks at the judge. "Nothing further your honor." He turns around swiftly and heads back to his table. He has all that he wants from me. All that he needs to add my brother to the system.

My brother's lawyer stands up. "We have no questions for the witness your honor."

James sits next to me on our way home in the car. I look over at him to see him staring out the window, his face full with concentration, as if he's thinking hard about something, something that the average fourteen-year-old wouldn't be thinking. I reach over and tap his arm.

"James," I say to him, which feels like the first time. "I'm not mad at you. I forgive you."

He just nods his head and looks back out the window.

**

When I was thirteen, my brother accidentally shot me.

**

Nine years has passed by since that incident. I am now twenty-two and in college. I sit in my room in my on-campus apartment watching TV. My cell phone rings. *James* appears on the Caller ID.

"Hello."

"Hey Sis,"

"Hey James."

We talk about how each other is doing, what we've been up to and more. He makes me laugh, as usual.

"I remember when we were in Rudgate…" he says reminiscing about our high school days. He talks about the fights that he, Noland and Javon got into. The girls he used to talk to. The trouble he use to get into and more.

He sighs. "Man, sometimes I wish I could go back to those times."

"I don't," I say frowning. "Those were dark days for me." I remember the times I slipped into a deep, dark depression. It was a time that I no longer desired to live (I never thought about committing suicide, but if a car just so happened to hit me when crossing the street then I was ok with that).

He gets quiet for a minute. "Yeah I know."

I don't say anything.

"You were always in yo room and to yourself."

"Yeah."

"But I knew why you were like that though."

We both know what he's talking about, but neither one of us say anything. We just leave it up in the air.

"Well sis, I was just checking up on you," he says after awhile. "I guess I'll talk to you later."

"Ok."

"I love you Sis."

"I love you too."

**

When I was thirteen, my brother accidentally shot me.

**

It's December 18, 2010 and I just graduated from college, Grand Valley State University to be exact. I'm on an emotional high. I just accomplished a very high milestone in my life and the feeling is exhilarating. But James wasn't there to celebrate with me. Due to some miscommunication, James and some others weren't able to make the graduation ceremony to see me walk.

"James is very upset," my auntie tells me.

I decide to call him.

"Hello," James' girlfriend says.

"Hey, is James there?"

"Oh Jana, he just left out."

"Oh ok, I was just calling him to see if he was ok."

"Yeah, he was really upset that he missed yo graduation. He kept saying 'Man, she's going to be so mad at me'."

"I'm not mad at him. I understood that it wasn't his fault."

"That's what I was telling him, but he just kept on saying it."

"Well, can you tell him that I called?"
"Yeah and congratulations."
"Thank you."

A few hours later James calls me back.
"Hey Sis, congratulations, I hope you not mad at me."
"Thank you. And I'm not mad at you, its fine. I'm not trippin' over it."
"I was mad that I missed yo big day."
"It's ok, James."
"But, I'm proud of you man. I really am."
"Thanks, James."
We continue to talk a little more, he makes me laugh, and then we say our goodbyes.
"I love you, Sis."
"I love you too, James."

I feel uneasy after I hang up from him. As if there was an unspoken emotion I was catching from him.
"It seems like he feels guilty," I say to my auntie. I go to her for everything. "And I feel like he's been carrying that around all the time."
"I get that feeling too," my auntie says. "And he probably does feel guilty for what happened."
"And we don't talk about that incident at all," I say frustrated. "We just ignore it."
"Well maybe y'all should."

I hang up from my auntie and call James back.
"Hey James," I say a little nervous. "I need to talk to you about something."

"Wasup."

"I've been getting this feeling that you've been carrying around this guilt about...you know, what happened."

He's silent for a moment. "I do feel guilty about what happened."

A female's intuition is everything. "You know I was never mad at you for what happened right?" Without my permission tears begin to fall. I can imagine the guilt that he's carrying around and the pain that it's causing him. I just want to make all of that go away.

"Yeah I know you wasn't, but still though, I felt really bad about what happened."

"Well, I was never mad. I knew that it was an accident and that you didn't mean it." We're silent for a moment. "I just feel like we never talk about it, you know."

"Yeah, but I talk about it all the time to my girlfriend. I tell her what happened and how I feel about it."

"Well that's good."

"Yeah."

"But we'll talk more about it later. I just had a feeling that you were feeling that way."

He laughs. "I knew out of everyone, *you* would be the one to know how I be feeling."

"Yeah," I laugh. It's always been that way with us. "But I'll talk to you later."

"Alright sis, love you."

"Love you too."

**

When I was thirteen, my brother accidentally shot me.

**

In March, James comes to stay with me, my auntie, and our little sister Autumn for a few weeks. It feels like old times. He and I talk and laugh like we use to. We spend our times at the public library, me doing my internship and writing, him applying for jobs and looking for employment.

"Hey James," I say after we made it home from the library. "I'm going to write a piece about you and me and how we never talk about me getting shot."

"Oh yeah?"

"Yeah, so I was thinking that maybe we should sit down and talk about it."

"I thought we already talked about it?" His demeanor says that he's really uncomfortable and doesn't want to talk about it.

"Yeah, just a little bit though." I back off a little. "Can I at least interview you?" I have a couple of questions to ask him.

"If it's for your story, then yeah I guess.

But I never get the chance to…

**

When I was thirteen, my brother accidentally shot me.

**

This was something that is often left unsaid, but as time goes on and I begin to heal I can say it.
When I was thirteen, my brother accidentally shot me.

But for my brother, it goes left unsaid.

This Scar of Mine

"*D*on't scratch too hard, don't scratch too hard. The scar might bust open if I scratch too hard,*"* I say to myself as I lightly run the tips of my fingernails up and down my stomach, the roughness and bumpiness of my scar reminds me of its fragility. I stare at my unclothed self in the bathroom mirror, my left arm subconsciously sliding over my stomach trying to hide the scar, even from me. Nine years and I still have trouble showing off my scar.

This scar of mine reminds me of "That situation" every time I look at it. As if it were a keepsake that I didn't *want* to *keep*.

"It's a symbol of strength," my auntie's voice rings through my head. But, for some reason, it's hard for me to see it that way.

"Don't scratch too hard, don't scratch too hard. The scar might bust open if I scratch too hard."

I wake up in a hospital room that is filled with "get well soon" cards, teddy bears and balloons. I can tell that this is a children's hospital. The paintings of giraffes and elephants on the walls give it away. The TV is on and the sound of cartoons plays in the background. Realization washes over me, what I thought was a dream has now become my reality. My thirteen-year-old self looks down to see staples running down the length of my stomach. *Staples*: a flimsy device that holds paper together. *Paper.* I try not to let fear appear on my face as I look over to my auntie who is looking at me. But I cannot help but to feel afraid. *Staples* are holding my stomach together.

"Good morning Jana`," my doctor greets me. He is followed by nurses and one other doctor. "How are you feeling today?"

"Ok," I say feebly. I'm far from ok though.

The doctor looks over my chart. "I'll tell ya, you are one lucky young lady." He looks up at me. "One minute later and you would've been dead, or at best, paralyzed."

"No," my auntie interjects. "She's blessed."

The doctor just looks at my auntie and smiles. "Well, let's take a look at that scar," he says returning his focus to me.

I lift up my shirt, a little self-conscious about what they're going to see. My doctor and the other both lean in to take a closer look.

"Ahh," the other doctor says. "That is beautiful." My doctor smiles with pride, but I am baffled by this comment.

"You see how I didn't go around the bellybutton, but through?" My doctor asks.

"Oh yes," the other doctor says pleased. "That is a remarkable job." They both lean away and my doctor flips through my chart.

"Well Jana`, it's seems like you're recovering very well."

I just nod my head.

"Now we did take out your appendix. It was completely shattered by the bullet," he goes on. "We've got most of the bullet out, but there is however a piece of it is still inside of you."

Fear becomes apparent on my face.

"It would've caused more damage to try to take it out than to keep it in," my doctor explains. "But there might be some symptoms like vomiting, etc."

"You'll be fine," my auntie says, reassuring me.

I slowly look down at my stomach that is lined up with staples. I imagine the fragment of the bullet inside my body, determined to be a part of me.

My doctor follows my gaze. "We've stitched up the inside of your stomach and they'll dissolve so we won't have to go back in to take them out," he explains. "And, as you can see, we've also stapled your stomach."

I still don't say anything. I just let all the information that he's giving me sink in.

"You should be fine Jana`," he says smiling at me. "You have a nice day."

I smile weakly and go back to looking at my stomach. Staples are lined up and down my stomach. I feel like a science experiment. Like a freak.

"Don't scratch too hard, don't scratch too hard. The scar might bust open if I scratch too hard."

I stare at my unclothed self in the bath room mirror, the tips of my fingers mindlessly running up and down my scar. I think about those staples running down my stomach and the marks they left behind. Nowadays when I look hard enough, I can still vaguely see the puncture marks that the staples left behind, 19. My fingers go over those vague marks.

I think about that piece of bullet that's still inside of me. Like the scar, that piece of the bullet will be a part of me forever. Sometimes I feel like Harold Crick from *Stranger than Fiction*, a piece of a foreign object inside of me due to a near death experience, but yet ironically keeping me alive.

"Don't scratch too hard, don't scratch too hard. The scar might bust open if I scratch too hard."

For a long time I've lied to people about the story of my scar.

At the age of fourteen, not even a year after I received my scar, I stand in the living room at a ninth grade friend's house. We're listening to music on the radio and one of my friends is showing me how to hip roll. I left up my shirt, revealing my stomach when I see all of them stare. There's a long moment of silence when I realize my mistake.

"What happened to you?" my friend Patricia asks, pointing at my stomach. I'm silent for a moment, thinking of my answer before I say it. Those who know me and know what happened to me all look at me differently. Pity lies behind their eyes, a look that constantly reads "You poor, poor girl." I hate that look.

"I got my appendix taken out." Which is partly true, but the real story behind my scar is much different.

They all just nod and accept my story. I begin to roll my hips to the music, secretly relieved that I didn't have to endure that pity look and a thousand questions.

"Don't scratch too hard, don't scratch too hard. The scar might bust open if I scratch too hard."

This scar of mine reminds me of the struggle that I've been through. The pain that I felt. The tears that I've shed. The straddling of sanity and insanity. Life and death. Reality and fantasy. And an infinite amount of other possibilities.

As I stare at my unclothed self in the bathroom mirror, the tips of my fingers mindlessly running up and down my scar, I think about my recovery during the summer of '01.

At the age of thirteen, it's hard for me to come to terms with the fact that I've been shot. I've had my brush with death and ended up escaping it. Just the fact that I am able to walk around and say "I've been shot and survived," is a hard thing for me to swallow.

It's hard for me to go back to the house where I was shot. So I go to stay at my stepmom's house for the summer. My recovery from the hospital is rough. Many nights I sit up crying while listening to Eminem's "Sing for the Moment." I'll sit there wondering why I was still here. As lyrics from Eminem flow through my headphones I sit there yearning for my mother and father. And as I lay down with tears flowing from my eyes, I wonder why God still has me here.

Occasionally I'll run my fingers up and down my scar.

"Don't scratch too hard, don't scratch too hard. The scar might bust open if I scratch too hard."

**This scar of mine keeps me motivated
to be better. To be successful.
Reminding me that every breath counts.
Every step I have to take.
And every strategy has to result with me
WINNING IN THE END.**

    As every second, every minute, every hour, every day, every week, every month, and every year goes by a part of me gradually gets better. A part of me slowly gets healed. A part of me progressively gets comfortable with my scar and the situation that got it there. My scar reminds me of the fragility of life. It reminds me of how at any given moment life can be taken away from you. So now I try to make the most of it. When I dream, I dream big because you only get one opportunity and you got to make it count.

    "Don't scratch too hard, don't scratch too hard. The scar might bust open if I scratch too hard."

    As I now, at 22-years-old, stare at my unclothed self in the bathroom mirror, the tips of my fingers mindlessly running up and down my scar, I think about that saying that I tell myself. My fingers mindlessly running up and down my scar, the roughness and bumpiness reminds me of its fragility. But as I think about it, my scar is not fragile. It's been nine years and my scar hasn't bust open on me yet. It has remained strong.

**This scar of mine represents strength.
Represents determination.
Represents sorrow. Represents
struggle. Represents success.
IT REPRESENTS ME.**

As I now, at 22-years-old, stare at my unclothed self in the bath room mirror, the tips of my fingers mindlessly running up and down my scar, I realize that the whole phobia of my scar busting open has become a metaphor.

"Don't scratch too hard, don't scratch too hard. The scar might bust open if I scratch too hard."

Whenever my scar itched I would just pat it or scratch it lightly, just barely touching the surface. And at the age of 13 through 16 whenever I was asked how I got my scar I would just tell them that I'd gotten my appendix taken out, just barely touching the surface. I've been running from the fact that I *was* shot and I *did* survive. For whatever reason, I've been ashamed of this.

"Don't scratch too hard, don't scratch too hard. The scar might bust open if I scratch too hard."

As I now, at 22-years-old, stare at my unclothed self in the bathroom mirror, my scar begins to itch. And now I begin to scratch. Not a pat or just a light scratch. I dig deep. Really making sure that the itch is gone and will think twice before it comes back. I am no longer ashamed to tell people how I got my scar.

"When I was thirteen I got shot," I'll tell them. And then I just smile once I see the shock written over their faces.

I finish scratching my scar and I continue to stare at my unclothed self in the bath room mirror.

"Ahh, that is beautiful," I remember the doctor say nine years back. And now as I look at my unclothed self in the mirror, I see that.

"It's a symbol of strength," my auntie's voice rings through my head. I now see it that way.

This scar *is* mine.